Spirituality:

The Meaning, Our Journey
and The True Path

Irmansyah Effendi, M.Sc.

Publisher
Natural Way of Living
PO Box 1470
JOONDALUP DC WA 6919
AUSTRALIA
www.naturalwayofliving.com

ISBN: 978-0-9945524-0-2

Because of the dynamic nature of the Internet, any web addresses or links contained in this book may have changed since publication and may no longer be valid. The views expressed in this work are solely those of the author and do not necessarily reflect the views of the publisher, and the publisher hereby disclaims any responsibility for them.

The author of this book does not dispense medical advice or prescribe the use of any technique as a form of treatment for physical, emotional, or medical problems without the advice of a physician, either directly or indirectly. The intent of the author is only to offer information of a general nature to help you in your quest for emotional and spiritual wellbeing. In the event you use any of the information in this book for yourself, which is your constitutional right, the author and the publisher assume no responsibility for your actions.

May all beings realize more about the real purpose of life and use the path that has been provided by the Creator.

Preface

We come across the word "spirituality" quite often in our daily lives, but for most people, spirituality is still something that is viewed as quite mysterious. People often associate all things related to the non-physical realm with spirituality. Collecting items such as ancient swords, antique crystals, meditating, learning or practicing non-physical disciplines are often also associated with spirituality.

Indeed, the scope in which spirituality is related to non-physical matters is vast. Hence the reason I wrote this book, **Spirituality: The Meaning, Our Journey and the True Path**, to share a clearer understanding with you about various matters that relate to spirituality.

In this book, we will begin by discussing the meaning of spirituality itself, the available options, and recognizing how each of those options should be categorized according to its direction and purpose. Subsequently, we will discuss spirituality in greater depth to gain a more profound understanding; that is, spirituality in relation to the true purpose of our lives.

Our life is a beautiful and important gift of love from the Creator. Therefore it is fundamental that we use our lives in accordance with the true purpose of life itself. Our lives will hold a much deeper value if we practice spirituality just for that purpose. So, in the majority of this book, we will discuss spirituality in line with the true purpose of life, how to do our best and so forth.

What I am sharing with you in this book is not intended to judge any particular group or discipline. As long as it is used for the good of others, every form of learning will certainly have its benefits. What is discussed in this book is simply intended to remind readers about the available options and to recommend practicing spirituality for matters that are in accordance with the true purpose of life, which is also the Will of the Creator.

I hope that after reading this book, those of you who are interested in mastering spirituality will be able to distinguish more clearly the meaning and the available choices. Then you will be in a position to ask yourself what it is that you really want to achieve and subsequently make the best choice according to your wish. For those of you unfamiliar with the notion of spirituality or those who are bewildered by it and wonder whether spirituality is something reserved for those who are attracted to non-physical matters, I hope that through reading this book, your questions will be answered.

This book is closely related to the book **The Real You: Beyond Forms and Lives** that discusses spirituality, our true self, the real purpose of life, and the best way to attain that purpose. While **The Real You: Beyond Forms and Lives** focuses on our spirit/true self, this book looks at spirituality from a more general point of view. You may read both books to obtain a more complete understanding about *spirituality; our true self, the real purpose of life* and how to best live your life for that real purpose.

Hopefully what I share in this book will be beneficial to you to better direct your whole heart and whole being to the Creator, to open your heart and surrender more to the Creator, our one and only destiny. At the same time, by opening our heart to the Creator, our relationship with others will improve because whether we realize it or not, the ego that prioritizes itself will become less dominant. The abundant blessings from the Creator will also help us in our endeavors and everything else in our lives, because the Creator is also the Source of Prosperity and All that is Best.

November 2013

Irmansyah Effendi

Table of Illustrations

Table of Contents

Chapter 1
The Understanding of "Spirituality"

The word "spirituality" stems from the word spirit which, according to the Oxford Dictionary, means *"the non-physical part of a person which is the seat of emotions and character; the soul"*. From this definition and the creation of its noun, spirituality, we can see how this word can be interpreted in vastly differing ways. Hence, matters related to the soul or spirit can all be associated with spirituality.

First of all, let us begin by understanding the meaning of soul and spirit. The soul and the spirit are not something strange. Indeed they form an integral part of all human beings. To clarify let us explore the three kinds of consciousness a human being has.

A. The Three Levels of Consciousness in a Human

In our daily lives, when we refer to a human being's center of consciousness, we tend to refer to the brain. Our brain is the center of our physical consciousness, that physically exists and forms a part of our physical body which we recognize the most in our day-to-day lives. It may be surmised that the brain, as the center of our physcial consciousness, is the part most widely recognized, studied and used.

Illustration 1: Common Understandings of Spirituality

Studies related to the brain are easily found in human anatomy books. Many books discuss the anatomy of the brain, how to improve our brain's capacity, and there are even books that examine diseases and other matters related to the brain. However, knowledge about our other kinds of consciousness are, by comparison, much scarcer.

In reality, as a human, we have three kinds of consciousness: the **brain**,

soul and **spirit**. The brain is the center of consciousness of the physical body. The other centers of consciousness, the soul and spirit, do not possess a physical form and are generally not as well known.

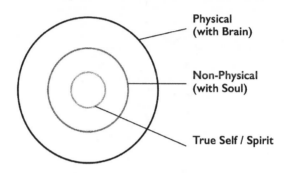

Illustration 2: The Three Human Consciousness While Still Alive

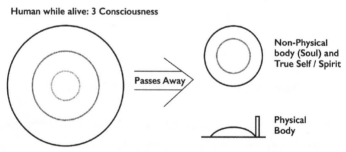

Illustration 3a: The Expiration of Physical Consciousness after Death and the Continuation of the Soul and Spirit Consciousness

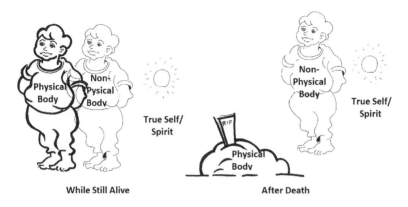

Illustration 3b: *A Human's Body and Consciousness During Life and After Death*

The soul and spirit are both centers of consciousness that exist in every human. These two consciousness are rarely acknowledged or talked about in comparison to the numerous discussions about the brain. This is a result of them not being a part of the physical body and our physical senses only being able to recognize physical matters. Even though both the soul and the spirit are non-physical, they nevertheless form parts of our being and have a significant influence on us. While the brain exists and is used only during the time we have our physical body, which is a temporary period of time whilst we are alive, the two other consciousness existed long before we were born, long before we were in our mothers' wombs and will continue to exist even after we die. The soul and the spirit are parts of us that existed long before we lived on earth, continue to exist while we are alive and will continue to exist after we die. However, the soul is not a consciousness that will remain with us for all eternity.

In ***Illustration 2***, I would like to show that the spirit is the deepest part within every human. The soul is the intermediary, while the outermost layer is what we recognize in our day-to-day lives as our physical body. In the previous illustrations *(Illustration 3a and 3b)* it is shown that even when the physical body ceases to exist, the non-physical body layers with the soul as the center of consciousness and the spirit still exist.

To further clarify the three different kinds of consciousness, let us review each consciousness briefly.

1. Brain

The brain is a part of the physical body, or more accurately the center of consciousness of the physical body that is located in our head. Scientifically speaking, there are several aspects we already understand about the brain, such as:

a. Consists of the right and left brain
b. The Center of thoughts/logic
c. Controls the nerves of the body

In our daily lives, we learn by utilizing our brain. Beginning with memorizing and processing information, making decisions (based on the knowledge within our brain), as well as considering the pros and cons of choices that we face. In truth, the majority of humans rely purely on their brains in their daily lives (even for important and special moments) despite the fact our brain has limitations.

2. Soul

Before discussing the soul, it is imperative to let you know that my use of the terms "soul" and "spirit" is opposite to how they may generally be used. For me, the soul is related to a part of a person who has died. Certain people can actually see the form of the soul – quite similar to when a person was still alive – even though the physical body has ceased to exist.

The form that resembles the physical body of the deceased is in fact the non-physical body layer, while the soul itself is the center of consciousness of the non-physical body. From one point of view, the non-physical form of a deceased person is still similar to when he or she was alive.

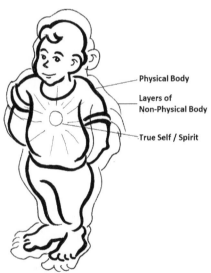

Illustration 4: *The Physical Body, the Non-Physical Body and the True Self of a Human*

Even though I have been referring to the soul and non-physical body layers in the context of someone who has passed away, the soul and non-physical body layers still exists in every human while they are alive.

However, those who tend to use only their brain and five senses – that can only sense physical things – seldom recognize the presence of their own non-physical being. You may have heard stories of people who, having lost a limb, say that often they feel the presence of "something" in the missing part of their body. What is that "something"? That is a part of their non-physical body layer. Our non-physical body layers always follow the movements of our physical body. However, when a person loses a part of their physical body such as fingers, toes, arms or legs, it does not mean that they have also lost their non-physical body. The non-physical body does not die. So, even though the physical body has ceased to exist, the non-physical body continues to exist.

Actually, every human possesses seven body layers. In *Illustration 4*, the non-physical body layers are shown on purpose as a single layer, because most people who have clairvoyant abilities can only see the smallest/coarsest non-physical body layer, which is the second body layer. The first body layer is the physical body that we know. The other six body layers, starting from the second to the seventh body layer, are all non-physical body layers: each layer is higher/bigger than the ones before it. So, for example, the third body layer is bigger than the second body layer *(See Illustration 5: The Human Physical Body and the 6 Non-Physical Body Layers).* The soul is the center of these non-physical body layers. Similar to the relationship between our brain and our physical body, our non-physical body has a consciousness that is called the soul. Further information about the soul can be read in **Soul Consciousness: An Effective Technique to Reach Your Higher Consciousness**, in which you can find simple methods to be conscious as your soul while you are still alive.

3. Spirit

The spirit is the true self of a person that resides within the heart. This very spirit is what we often refer to as the spark of the Creator. The spirit does not have a form, not even a non-physical one. Even though the spirit is not physical, the spirit is beyond what we refer to as the non-physical. There are no human words accurate enough to explain such divine matters.

Because our spirit is our true self, instead of saying we are sparks of the "Creator," it is more accurate to say that we are sparks of our "True Source" as we are referring to the True Source of our true self.

Illustration 5: *The Physical Body and the 6 Non-Physical Body Layers of a Human*

Our spirit or true self is the spark of True Source that resides within our heart. That is why our heart is often referred to as the "key of our connection to True Source". Without using the heart, we will not be able to communicate properly with True Source. As "True Source" is a general term, unaffiliated to any particular group or religion, we will use this terminology to refer to the Creator in this book as it reminds us of our real relationship as the spark of the Source. More information on how to use our heart can be found in **Smile to Your Heart Meditation: Simple Practices for Peace, Health, and Spiritual Growth.**

B. The Subconscious

To complete our discussion about the human consciousness, I have added a section elaborating about the subconscious. Some people, even those who are involved in the field of human consciousness, may confuse the subconscious with our higher consciousness. Some even label the higher consciousness as the "subconscious". This stems from a limited understanding, either because of the shortage of available references or their limited experience. Those who endeavor to attain their higher levels of consciousness often instead experience their subconscious which leads them to make the assumption that the higher consciousness belongs in the subconscious world.

The subconscious *is not* a consciousness; rather we may consider it as a "trash can" in which all the excess information from other levels of consciousness is discarded. This excess information is caused by over- thinking or dwelling on a subject, which often happens at the level of our brain and soul. So the subconscious does not have the ability to obtain information from our soul consciousness, which is a higher consciousness. That is why many people assume that if they can access their subconscious and find information that originated from the soul consciousness, they have attained their higher consciousness. Unfortunately, they have not.

As a trash can and not a consiousness, the subconscious has the ability to store information. However, it is incapable of gaining realizations from an experience. An example of a realization might be when we choose to pray even though we're feeling lazy, and are able to feel the beauty of choosing to be closer to the Creator. That feeling is what we refer to as a realization. This realization can only be experienced and realized by the brain, soul or spirit, but not our subconscious.

C. What is Spirituality?

Let us now return to the understanding of the word spirituality. Essentially, spirituality is everything related to our own spirit and soul. Even though these parts are non-physical and cannot be recognized by our five senses, they are all a part of us and exist within us every moment. They even existed long before we were born and will continue to exist after our death. All practices, lessons and other things related to our spirit and soul can also be referred to as spiritual matters. For example, practices to cleanse the *chakras* (our non-physical energy doors), meditation, and even prayers can be considered as a part of spirituality.

However, commonly in practice the word spirituality is not used exclusively in relation to matters concerning the spirit and soul. Other things that cannot be recognized by the five senses are often also attached to spirituality. That is why we should be clearer and more specific when we mention the term spirituality.

10

Doing something positive for one particular consciousness does not necessarily mean that we are doing something that will advance the others

One thing that is important and essential to know, especially for those of us who are seeking spiritual advancement, is: what are you really looking for? Although all three consciousnesses reside together within our one being, doing something positive for one particular consciousness does not necessarily mean that we are doing something that will advance the others. As an example, if our brain is studying mathematics, this does not mean that the spirituality of our soul or spirit is advancing. This is why I have written this book and it is my hope that reading this book can complement your resources. Particularly, in relation to another book I have written titled **The Real You: Beyond Forms and Lives.** This will help you have a deeper understanding of these discussions, so that when the opportunity arises, you will be able to make the best choice.

Chapter 2
Fundamental Knowledge within "Spirituality"

Before we delve into deeper discussions about spirituality, let us begin with the most fundamental knowledge there is about it. Without this understanding, we risk muddling up different spiritual aspects that are completely unrelated.

In this chapter we will discuss fundamentally important matters that relate to spirituality including:

- Humans are More than Just the Physical and Non-Physical
- Different Aspects of the Non-Physical Realm
- Divine Matters are Beyond the Non-Physical
- The Soul and its Non-Physical Body Layers
- The Spirit does not Have a Form
- Soul vs. Spirit

A. Humans are More than Just the Physical and Non-Physical

As previously mentioned, humans have three kinds of consciousness: brain, soul, and spirit. However, I must mention that many people perceive humans to be made of just two parts: the physical and the non-physical. This is understandable, as most people do not recognize non-physical matters in their daily lives. Therefore, if something is invisible to our physical sight it remains unknown and unrecognized. As a consequence, obtaining a deeper understanding or proper categorization of this invisible matter becomes almost impossible.

In our previous discussions, we have briefly reviewed the differences between our spirit and our soul. Although both the spirit and soul, from the perspective of our physical brain, can be considered as non-physical, the spirit and the soul are completely different. Remember that the spirit is the spark of True Source, while the soul and the non-physical body layers are just the intermediary between the spirit and the brain. What follows now will clarify the differences between various non-physical matters for you.

B. Different Aspects of the Non-Physical Realm

Most people will divide human existence into two categories: the physical and the non-physical. For example, some assume that when a person who has performed many good deeds during their lifetime passes away, they will meet God. This perception – physical and non-physical- is illustrated in *Illustration 6* as follows.

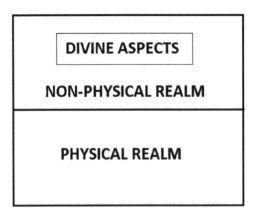

Illustration 6: *A Common Categorization of Everything that Exists (A Misconception)*

This perception is not entirely correct because it is only seeing it from one perspective. Scientifically speaking, this perspective or division is often referred to as a dimension. If you are interested in further reading specifically about dimensions, you can read books related to quantum physics. In this book, I will only touch briefly on dimensions.

Spiritually speaking, multiple dimensions are considered to exist. The exact number of dimensions varies from the perception of one school of thought to another. The lowest dimension, with the lowest frequency, is often referred to as the first dimension. The dimension just one level above is referred to as the second dimension and the one after that, is referred to as the third dimension and so on. The most important thing for us to know is that all physical matters, such as our physical body and all physical objects that we know of on earth, as well as on other planets, are considered a part of the third dimension. As our five senses are part of the physical body, a part of the physical dimension otherwise known as the third dimension, we are only able to recognize matters that exist in the third dimension. Anything that originates from a dimension other than the third dimension is unrecognizable to our five physical senses. That is why, all things that exist in a different dimension, whether it be an object or a living creature, are often referred to as non-physical elements.

Senses from a certain dimension are only able to recognize matters from that same dimension. If you pay attention while speaking to those who have clairvoyant abilities, you may recognize that some talk about souls, others about chakras or energy, and others talk about other matters. This is because the non-physical eyes of those with clairvoyant abilities are only opened for certain dimensions and therefore can only see matters from that dimension in which their non-physical eyes are opened.

There are those who have several non-physical eyes opened so they can see matters from multiple dimensions where their non-physical eyes are opened. However, those of you who use your logic may begin to wonder, if there are hundreds of dimensions, is it possible for someone to have hundreds of non-physical eyes? The answer is no. We have a limited number of non-physical eyes. So, even if every single one of a person's non-physical eyes were opened, they could still only see matters from a relatively limited amount of dimensions. No one is capable of seeing everything in every dimension.

Our brain is limited to the third dimension. That is why it may not be easy for most brains to comprehend matters that exceed three dimensions. On this earth there are also matters that do not originate from the third dimension, because of inter-dimensional overlap. We do not need to look too far, just go back to our previous discussion about our spirit and non-physical body layers. Where are they? They are within our body, on earth, but they are not from this third dimension. So, at any particular place, there may be matters that are made up of various dimensions. This is what I mean by inter-dimensional overlap.

C. Divine Matters are Beyond the Non-Physical

In addition, there is a very important matter we need to be aware of. Among non-physical matters, there are things that may appear to be non-physical from our physical perspective but in fact should not be described as non-physical. They belong in the Divine Realm. Everything in the divine realm is beyond the non-physical. To ease your understanding, refer to *Illustration 7* below.

For your notes, this illustration serves to emphasize the difference between Divine matters and other non-physical matters. This Illustration does not reflect the positioning of dimensions as I have previously mentioned.

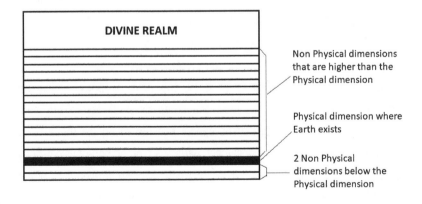

Illustration 7: *Physical, Non-Physical, and Divine Matters*

D. The Soul and its Non-Physical Body Layers

When we discuss the soul, we must also discuss the non-physical body layers, as the two are closely related. Remember that our soul is the center of consciousness of our non-physical body layers. It is similar to the relationship between our brain and our physical body.

Let us now consider our non-physical body that consists of different layers *(See Illustration 5: The Human body with its 6 non-physical body layers)* and non-physical matters that belong in different dimensions. It is now time to discuss the existence of our different body layers in different dimensions. Please refer to the explanation below:

1. The First Body Layer: The Physical body that we know, is located in the third dimension
2. The Second Body Layer: Non-Physical, in the fourth dimension.
3. The Third Body Layer: Non-Physical, in the fifth dimension.
4. The Fourth Body Layer: Non-Physical, in the sixth dimension.
5. The Fifth Body Layer: Non-Physical, in the seventh dimension.
6. The Sixth Body Layer: Non-Physical, in the eighth dimension.
7. The Seventh Body Layer: Non-Physical, in the ninth dimension.

So, other than the first body layer, the physical body, which we recognize in our day-to-day lives, the other six body layers are non-physical. Our five physical senses cannot see nor recognize these other six body layers and their constituent parts. Our other non-physical body layers are located in the fourth to ninth dimensions. So, if even if all of our non-physical senses function completely, we would only be able to recognize non-physical matters in those dimensions.

Many people claim to have seen angels and other holy beings. Nevertheless, if you read holy books thoroughly, there are written warnings about being careful if we see or encounter angels. There are many naughty beings that like to disguise themselves as angels. If we merely rely on our non-physical sight, it is possible to be tricked. Only with our heart can we recognize the real truth. In addition, if we read many holy books carefully we learn that not everyone has the privilege to meet angels. Only prophets and messengers of True Source have met with the real angels. Why is it that the heart, and only the heart, can recognize the truth? We will discuss this shortly.

Let us return to the discussion related to our body layers and dimensions. Our physical body is in the third dimension. In the two lower dimensions, the first and second dimensions, there are various life forms whose bodies have a lower frequency compared to our physical body in the third dimension. Likewise, in each dimension above the ninth dimension, there are also various kinds of life forms whose frequency is higher. Everything in a higher dimension, whether an object or a living being, has a higher frequency than objects or living beings in a lower dimension. However, we will not discuss objects or living forms in these various dimensions because, as mentioned above, no parts of us exist in dimensions other than the third to the ninth.

E. The Spirit Does not Have a Form

Our spirit does not have a form at all. It is not easy to recognize our spirit because there is no practice that we can ever do that will connect us or give access to our spirit. There are only a handful of people who truly understand about the spirit. Further information about the spirit can be found in: **The Real You: Beyond Forms and Lives.**

F. Soul vs. Spirit

The next most important matter that we need to know is the difference between the spirit and all of the non-physical body layers. The spirit is not a part of the soul. The spirit is beyond the soul and is not a part of any of the non-physical body layers. If our highest body layer is within the ninth dimension, and there are hundreds of dimensions in total in this existence, our spirit is beyond all the dimensions that exist. Remember that our spirit is the *"dzat"* (spark) of The Creator. Our spirit belongs in the Divine Realm, higher and beyond ordinary non-physical matters.

Other than this difference, there are several other significant differences between the soul and the spirit. If you understand non-physical matters, you can actually access the non-physical body layers and the soul using simple methods. For example, if you wish to move the hand of your second body layer, all you need is to have the intention. Quite a few people have a relatively good connection with their non-physical body layers and their soul whether they use this to activate the senses from their non-physical body layers or for other purposes.

However, even though our spirit resides within us and is always with us, we are unable to access our spirit easily. Remember that our spirit is the "spark" of True Source. **True Source personally placed our spirit within our hearts.** We cannot and should not do anything to our spirit. Should we recklessly insist on doing something to our spirit, there will definitely be negative consequences.

It is important to note that our spirit is not something to be played around with. Numerous holy books also clearly mention this. So, we should not use the "senses" of our spirit or anything of our spirit. True Source has given us a different facility, our heart. Only with our heart can we recognize, not only all non-physical matters irrespective of which dimension they are in, but also all things beyond all dimensions. More importantly, with our hearts, we are able to distinguish non-physical matters that may otherwise be deceptive. In other words, things that "seem" or "feel" a certain way, may not be what they appear to be. Instead, what we see or feel could be something deceptive that is made up by other beings. Once again, only our hearts can recognize the truth. Whichever other senses we have are very likely to be tricked by those illusory things.

Many people muddle up or misconnect the soul and the spirit. They assume that if they cleanse the soul they will automatically cleanse the spirit. Or, if the soul attains the highest place, so will the spirit. These assumptions are not correct. The cleansing of the soul is not related to the cleansing of the heart or spirit. There may be times when the cleansing of the soul may help us to be prepared so the cleansing of the heart and spirit can happen more properly. Unfortunately, most people do not know this fact. Many people engage in cleansing or doing practices for their soul assuming that this cleansing will be beneficial for their whole being, including their spirit. However, from what we have discussed above, cleansing or positive things can happen on the spirit **only through the heart**. Without going through the heart, the spirit will not advance.

If we recklessly insist on doing something to our spirit, there will definitely be negative consequences

Why does cleansing of the soul not automatically benefit the heart or at least make the heart cleaner? Because our heart needs to open first, and only True Source Love can cleanse our heart and give all the good things to our heart. Cleansing of the soul cannot cleanse the heart. However, cleansing of the heart can automatically help cleansing of the spirit and the soul. We will discuss this further in the chapter about the heart.

Chapter 3
Our Journey

A long, long time ago before anything existed (The Earth, Heaven, The Universe and everything within it), each one of True Source *'sparks'* was in its original existence, that is the spirit. Our spirits left True Source. True Source, the All Loving, wanted to bring us back, but our spirit rejected; our spirit did not want to accept True Source Love.

Since our spirits did not want to accept the help and Love from True Source, True Source created another us to go through various lives and events so that, one day, we will be able to accept True Source Love and help in order to be brought back to True Source. That is why True Source bestowed every single one of the spirits, who left, a different consciousness and life form. In this life we identify it as the physical body.

We also need to know that the human form is just one among many forms of consciousness bestowed by True Source to True Source sparks.

There is a multitude of forms, but we will not discuss that in this book. Just for your information, other than humans there are also angels. What most people are unaware of is that angels are not in spirit form. Remember that spirits do not have forms, while we recognize that angels have forms, although they are non-physical.

Let us return to the subject of our human form. Everything needs time and process. A seed – let's say a mango seed – starts to grow and becomes a small seedling that takes many years to transform into a big and strong tree that can blossom and bear fruit. Imagine if that small seedling, when it is only several centimeters high, starts to bear fruit; that seedling will snap and die.

Similarly to the incarnation process itself, not only did our spirit need time to gain the ability to use this physical body, but life at the level of the physical body also needed to go through the evolution process. History teaches us that prior to the past two thousand years, most humans on Earth did not recognize that there is only one God. Most of them worshipped various deities *(polytheism)*.

It is only in the past two thousand years that humans have begun to recognize that there is only one God. It is not my intention to categorize either specific religions or beliefs. I would only like to show that every individual's preference of religion and beliefs is different depending on each of their personal experiences. From my own experience, and I really believe so, God really exists, but it is up to us, whether we are still busy with our concepts and habits or we are willing to follow our hearts to remember our Creator. To be fair, how can someone who doesn't know The Creator be able to choose The Creator?

True Source knew that we would need time and that one lifetime would not be enough. This resulted in the need for a form of 'bookkeeping'. Other than that, the physical body, or whatever form we were given for learning, is significantly different compared to the spirit, making it necessary to have an intermediary. For these two requirements, we need the non-physical body layers along with the center of its consciousness, which we identify as the soul.

Now, let us see the journey that the soul has been through from the perspective of spirituality. The souls of every human, irrespective of who they are, have been through a similar journey even though each one may not be exactly the same. We may have had different roles, but every soul has experienced various roles, in a variety of time and places, to achieve the same true purpose.

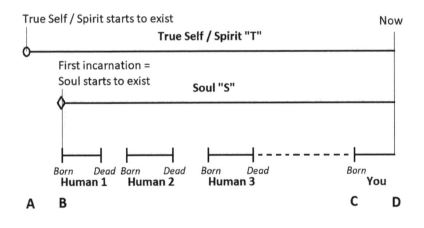

Illustration 8: *Our Journey*

In **Illustration 8**, I would like to show you several matters related to the journey of our three kinds of consciousness – the spirit, soul and physical body. At the beginning, at Point A, we were only just spirits; we did not have the non-physical body layers along with the soul nor the physical body. This is the time between the creation of our spirit by True Source, our spirit leaving True Source and the moment we started our very first incarnation (Point B).

So, point B is when we started to have our first incarnation. To make matters simpler to understand, in this illustration I have named the first incarnation as 'Human 1', even though our form during that incarnation may not have been human. The moment our spirit started its first incarnation, we were 'given' our non-physical body layers along with the soul as the center of its consciousness. We were also given the heart, together with the form that incarnates (in the illustration above, we can assume that incarnation to be as a human). After Point B, the spirit, which is our true self, our heart, and the non-physical body layers (with the soul as its consciousness) remain together, while our incarnations begin with the birth and end with the death of that form. The cycle of being born and dying continues itself repeatedly until we are born into our current lifetime. I marked this point with 'Point C', and this present moment at Point D.

So, the journey of each lifetime is only a small part of the entirety of the full journey. I have provided **Illustration 9** below (Incarnation as a human) to clarify this matter. The true purpose of life is not easily achieved. The spirit still needs further experiences and learning and needs to be reborn in the next form. That is why, after the "holiday" period, whether the soul goes to heaven, to a good place, or a bad place, the soul along with the spirit, must be reborn (incarnate).

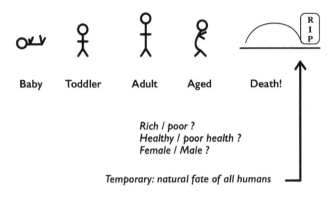

| Baby | Toddler | Adult | Aged | Death! |

Rich / poor ?
Healthy / poor health ?
Female / Male ?

Temporary: natural fate of all humans

Illustration 9: *Incarnation as a Human*

A. Form at Birth

The human form is not the only form provided by True Source. Nevertheless, it has clearly been mentioned in various holy books that the human form has the highest priority and provides the best opportunity to choose True Source and to become closer to True Source. Because of that, it would be so wonderful if we could let go our own expectations of our physical body and our condition. For example, expectations such as having a taller body, bigger eyes, to be more successful and so on. Being born as a human is already beyond all blessings. We must be grateful to True Source.

Almost all spirits begin their incarnation with a non-physical form. This matter is closely related to the process of creation of the whole existence. The learning places in the non-physical dimensions are more readily prepared compared to those in our dimension, i.e. this physical universe.

In addition, we also know that this Earth is relatively young. Scientists estimate our Earth to be around 4.6 billion years old, while our galaxy is around 13.7 billion years old.

So, while the Earth, which is very important for our spiritual growth, is still being prepared, simultaneously, our spirit is undergoing various preparations to be able to use the physical body in the best way possible. The Spirit usually begins its early incarnations in non-physical forms, then in simple physical forms and gradually is able to use more complicated forms, before finally being able to use the human body.

Non-Physical forms   Simple Physical forms   Human forms

Illustration 10: *Changes of Forms in Incarnations*

Even though the Earth has been inhabited for a long time, it does not mean that every spirit has had the chance to incarnate as a human on Earth. Some spirits are still incarnating in a different forms and places.

Furthermore, related to changes of forms in incarnations **(Illustration 10)**, in the event that somebody commits terrible deeds, he or she may be relegated to a lower form in a following incarnation. If his or her deeds were only slightly negative, then only the condition and surroundings are adjusted, without any changes to their form.

B. Spiritual Advancement in Incarnations

As we have begun discussing spirits who do bad deeds, we need to understand that the spiritual journey of our spirit is not like the course of our earthly education (school). On Earth, we learn about various topics, take exams and graduate to a higher level to learn more advanced lessons.

If we simply look at this Earth we can see that it is itself an enormous classroom, where classes of various levels are not separated/divided. The level of learning depends on what each human is experiencing.

The advancement level of the spirit that is within the soul may fluctuate. For example, the spirit may advance or worsen with each lifetime. As there are no labels for levels for the soul, the progress of the spirit and soul in an incarnation can be seen based on the 'holiday', meaning those souls who reach heaven at the end of their incarnation are advancing, while souls that end up in hell are performing poorly.

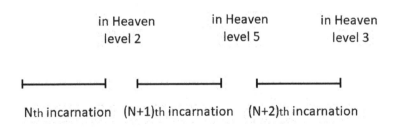

Illustration 11: "Holidays" at the End of Different Incarnations.

However, we must also be cautious in this matter, as we can see in **Illustration 11** above. So, for example, after incarnation N ends, the soul reaches heaven level 2; this is already something wonderful. At the end of the next incarnation (that we label N+1), the soul advanced even further and reached heaven level 5, meaning that the soul is progressing and doing well. Yet, at the end of the subsequent incarnation (that we label N+2), the soul only reached heaven level 3. Even though this particular soul has reached a relatively high level, which is level 3, higher than at Incarnation N, it is not as good as it was at the end of incarnation N+1. If at the end of incarnation N+1 the soul has reached heaven level 5, but only reached heaven level 3 at the end of incarnation N+2, spiritually speaking the condition of that soul has worsened.

Whatever and wherever that role is played out during an incarnation, the summary of everything is reflected in our heart attitude towards True Source. At the end of lifetime N, the heart attitude was quite good so that the related being could accept True Source Blessing that brought him/her to heaven level 2. At the end of lifetime N+1, the heart attitude improved so that he or she could accept True Source Blessing to bring him or her to heaven level 5. At the end of lifetime N+2, the heart attitude **worsened**, because that person could only accept True Source Blessing to bring him or her to heaven level 3, even though previously they had attained heaven level 5.

If you feel that this explanation is strange, do not look too far. This can be related to our own soul that has been through its previous journeys. Although we are discussing the summary of each lifetime, let us look at shorter periods of time. Recognize that we are still doing the same thing. There are days where we are diligent and wholehearted in becoming closer to True Source, but it usually doesn't last long. Afterwards, there are days where we become lazy or we are not as wholehearted anymore. It is time to recognize that we have been doing this for too long, to change this bad habit and to wholeheartedly do the best in choosing True Source.

C. True Source has Given Everything

As I have now referred to heaven repeatedly, I feel that I need to be frank. At the end of a lifetime, reaching heaven or hell, is not based on the good deeds that a soul has done during its lifetime. I am fully aware that what I am saying is very different to what most of you have understood all this time, but this is the truth.

True Source is the All Loving and is always giving what's best for us. So, every time someone passes away, True Source gives Abundant Blessings of Love that can bring that soul to the best place. However, souls that have a lot of burdens, attachments, desires and so forth are usually too busy and confine themselves in their busy-ness. If their heart is not opened enough, souls that have performed a lot of good deeds during their lifetime may be unable to recognize/see the Blessing of Love from True Source that manifests as a Light that brings souls to a beautiful place. Only souls whose hearts are sufficiently open can recognize that Light. Depending on the level of surrendering of the heart to True Source, the soul will let the Beautiful Light Blessing from True Source bring it to the best place.

Nevertheless, please be careful when reading this part. It does not mean that we do not need to pray or do good deeds. That is not what I mean at all. We still need to pray, give charity and perform good deeds for others, but without any expectation of receiving anything in return from True Source. Isn't being sincere in our actions very important? If we are aware that being sincere is important, this should not only be applied to our relationships with others, but also to our relationship with True Source. You may wonder, what is then the purpose of praying, giving charity and performing good deeds? The answer is to only choose, prioritize and surrender more and more to True Source; that is the best. Doing something with the expectation of receiving something in return from True Source will greatly reduce and hinder our surrendering to True Source.

To give you a clearer picture, I will also add the following explanations below:

- The Relationship between the physical body and the soul
- The Relationship between the soul and the spirit
- The Soul as a bookkeeper
- The Relationship between the spirit and the heart

D. The Relationship Between the Physical Body and the Soul

As the physical body and the spirit are two very different existences, an intermediary is needed. Experiencing various lifetimes over again on Earth or in other learning dimensions, where the law of action and reaction exists, creates the need for a form of bookkeeping. Because of this, an intermediary and a bookkeeper becomes necessary, which are both roles assigned to our non-physical body layers with the soul as its center of consciousness.

So, the non-physical body layers and the soul of a human are only together with the human when he or she is still alive. The presence of the soul within the physical body is the "essence of life" in a human. As soon as a human dies, then the non-physical body layers along with the soul will be separated from that physical body forever. The soul usually enters the physical body when the physical body is still within the mother's womb at about 3.5 months. However, depending on numerous factors, the soul may enter the fetus earlier or later. For example, the soul usually enters the physical body earlier in the case of babies with physical deformities.

31

E. The Relationship Between the Soul and the Spirit

The soul is the center of consciousness of the non-physical body layers and also acts as the intermediary and the bookkeeper of the journey of the spirit, as it experiences one lifetime after another before attaining the true purpose of life.

In a similar way to how the soul is the "essence of life" for the physical human body, so is the spirit to the soul. The Spirit is the "essence of life" of the soul. Without the spirit, the soul will cease to exist. Because of that, the spirit is always within the soul. When a human is still alive, the spirit is always together with the soul and the physical body. After death, wherever the soul goes, so does the spirit as the spirit always remains within the soul.

Unlike the human body whose lifetime is limited, our soul will always be together with us throughout our journey. The spirit will only separate from the soul when the final purpose is achieved; that is, when the spirit returns completely to The Creator. At that moment, the spirit will separate from the soul. The spirit returns to the Creator, while the soul returns to become a part of True Source Love again.

F. The Soul as a Bookkeeper

Human birth provides an opportunity for the soul to learn. However, every one of our actions creates a reaction,[1] a concept that is commonly referred to as *karma*. The reactions to our actions are always present and do not disappear after death. Everything will be brought forward to the next lifetime and so on. That is why those who are aware of this matter, seek to perform good deeds in their lifetime (often referred to as *dharma*) to reduce their negative karma from this lifetime and previous lifetimes. Our spirit itself is not

32

affected by our karma and only gains realizations about the meaning of prioritizing True Source.

I created *Illustration 12* to help you understand karma better. In this illustration, we created the analogy of a spirit who is experimenting with making sweet tea. The spirit does not finish the drink after every experiment but only tastes it. The glass being used represents the human body, while the water represents the soul.

TEA MAKING EXPERIMENT

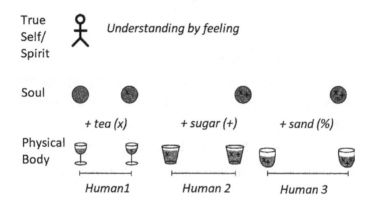

Illustration 12: The Soul Stores all Experiences From all Lifetimes

---

[1] In Spirituality, this is also often referred to as karma, the fruits of our actions. Karma is not something strange and is actually widely known by the general public. As proof, blow a piece of paper. See what happens. Can you see that the piece of paper moves? This proves that for every action, there will always be a reaction. Planes, boats and everything else can move because of this law of action-reaction. Wherever and whenever, this law of action-reaction will always happen, even though sometimes the reactions from several matters are not tangible. Usually, the reactions from positive actions are called positive karma, and reactions from negative actions are called negative karma.

At the beginning, the water was pure without any additional elements. Then, the spirit adds some tea to the water. The water turns into tea. When the next glass is used, we are already starting with the previous content that has already turned into tea. Next, if sugar is added to the second glass, then the content becomes sweet tea. Then as we move to another glass, we are starting with sweet tea for the tea and the sugar has dissolved within the water. If we now add sand in the third glass, then the content becomes sandy sweet tea. When we move this content to the next glass, we will start again with sandy sweet tea.

This analogy demonstrates several matters. At the beginning, our soul was like that pure water, with no karma whatsoever. But, as soon as we do anything that action will enter and dissolve into the water permanently. We can say that the spirit conducting the experiments only tastes in order to know and understand the result of each experiment. And for sure, if the spirit recognizes a mistake in its experiment (in this case, putting in sand), then the spirit must filter that sand out of the water. Without being filtered, the sand will not be removed on its own.

G. The Relationship Between the Spirit and the Heart

Do you remember what we discussed at the beginning of this chapter? Our spirits left True Source. The Almighty and All Loving tried to help us to return. But our spirit rejected the help from True Source. As our spirit rejected the direct help from True Source, True Source created another us that one day will be able to choose True Source. Let's say that right now in this lifetime as a human, we choose True Source. However, the part of us that chooses or wants to choose is our brain.

34

How can we use our brain in choosing True Source, so that True Source can help our spirit?

Let us refer to **Illustration 13** below. Remember that our spirit resides within our heart. True Source created our heart in such a way that we cannot do anything to our heart. Only True Source Love can help our heart. This understanding is important because we should also not do anything to our spirit. Our spirit left True Source because our spirit did too many things and refused to surrender to True Source. That is why our heart was created by True Source specifically to improve this condition. We may be able to improve ourselves but we cannot improve our heart or spirit. Only by surrendering to True Source can our heart and spirit be helped by True Source Love.

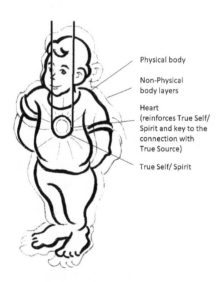

Physical body

Non-Physical
body layers

Heart
(reinforces True Self/
Spirit and key to the
connection with
True Source)

True Self/ Spirit

*Illustration 13: Our Heart is the Fortress as well as our Key
Connection to True Source*

Only by surrendering to True Source can our heart and our spirit be helped by the Love

A brain that is willing to accept True Source Love is a good starting point. However, if we do not use our heart, we will not be able to connect to our spirit. True Source Love can only help our spirit in moments when we use our heart. This is why the importance of using the heart is mentioned in various holy books.

The heart is an important key in our relationship with our own spirit. Generally speaking, the heart can be referred to as the key connection of every being to True Source. Meanwhile, as I have previously mentioned, only True Source Love can do positive things to our spirit.

Every time our heart is connected to True Source, our spirit, which is our true self, will advance because True Source always gives us Abundant Love. The problem is that we rarely use our hearts, which is the one and only key to accepting True Source Love. So, the more often we use our heart, the more we can accept True Source Love. To be able to accept True Source Love, we need to surrender more to True Source.

Any cleansing that is done to the spirit must only be done through the heart. We can say that all processes related to the spirit **must** be done through the heart, which is the facility to be helped directly by True Source. The spirit and the heart are closely interrelated. A cleaner heart can make the spirit cleaner too. Likewise, when a spirit has become cleaner or more

36

advanced, the heart will also become cleaner. We will discuss this matter further in **The First Key in Using the Heart** located in **Chapter 10.**

Chapter 4
Before Birth
and After Death

After seeing the broad outline of the journey that the three human consciousness have experienced *(refer to Illustration 8)*, let us now look at the journey in more detail. As we have already discussed what happens between Point A and B, next let us see what happens between Point B and C. We begin with the planning of life before birth (incarnation begins).

A. Planning of Life before Birth

Babies are born every second in all corners of the world; four babies are born per second to be exact. (http://www.ecology.com/birth.death.rates/). Some are female, some are male, with a plethora of varying physical conditions, from a huge diversity of families and in different places. You can be sure that every single one will experience his or her own unique journey. Our soul, together with our spirit within, cannot simply choose whichever form it desires. This choice is made in a special dimension, usually referred to as the *planning dimension*.

In the planning dimension, a dimension above all learning dimensions, the soul together with its guide will discuss various matters, including what the soul did in its past life, recognizing mistakes, weaknesses, positive matters and so on. Based on the individual's needs, the lessons that need to be learnt will be determined. These may include overcoming arrogance, loving others and other matters such as the estimated time of birth. Numerous babies are born on this earth every minute and therefore there are plenty of choices for physical bodies (babies) that can experience the necessary lessons within the desired time frame. The soul and the spirit cannot choose the physical body (baby) according to their own will. The guide will usually have to assess the deeds of the soul in its past lifetimes. Based on the deeds of each soul's past lifetime, several choices will be deemed appropriate for the physical body (baby) to be used by the soul and the spirit to learn, according to the necessary lessons in the desired time frame.

Based on the deeds of each soul's past lifetime, several choices will be deemed appropriate for the physical body (baby) to be used by the soul and the spirit to learn.

The choices given in the planning dimension are different to the concept of our limited mind. Remember that the lesson is the main priority. The priority in making the choice is based on the time frame and necessary lessons. The available choices are then adjusted according to each individual's karma in his or her past lifetimes. In general, we can say that a person enjoying pleasant conditions in their life on earth is a consequence of the positive effect of giving charity and performing good deeds in their past lives. However, those who have difficulties in bearing children, for example, can be related to what they did to their own children or other children in their past.

Illustration 14: *Choosing Options of Different Lives in the Planning Dimension*

Occupying positions of power does not necessarily mean that the soul or spirit has reached a high spiritual level. Souls/spirits at a more advanced level tend to be born in more remote locations or problems places because they will be able to help those who need it directly. Those souls/spirits will usually not tend to choose roles related to power.

From this point of view, we can also see that True Source is infinitely just. Without this knowledge, some humans may question (or protest) why it is that their physical body or other worldly aspects are not as good when they compare themselves to others. The answer is now clear; every current condition is related to what we did in our past lifetimes.

Even though souls usually interact directly with each of their guides, decisions related to choices of physical body/form/life that the soul can choose, are not made by the direct guide. The direct guides only convey the available choices given by the council of elders in the planning dimension, whilst the council of elders acquires those decisions based on True Source Will.

The soul is given the opportunity to 'peek' at several aspects of the available choices – this is why we often experience what is commonly called *déjà vu*. Here, although the individual had never experienced that event it was shown briefly to the individual's soul when the soul was still in the planning dimension. More accurately, at the time the soul was given several choices of different lives.

Illustration 14 shows that the soul can see several aspects from each given choice, including the physical body and several important matters that will be experienced by each choice.

After the soul has made a choice from the available options, the guide will help the soul to realize important lessons that the soul will encounter, discuss important matters thoroughly together with the soul, while comparing the things the soul has done in the past lifetimes. After everything is clear and the time of birth is approaching, the soul will be brought to a special place to be given a special briefing by several elders, adjusted according to the level of the soul being briefed. At the time, the soul will be given special advice that will help the soul in the lifetime that it is going to experience. After this, the soul is 'ready', and only needs to wait for its time to be (re)born.

When the fetus is about 3.5 months in the mother's womb, True Source Love will deliver the soul and spirit to enter the body of the fetus. The baby is then born and will experience life as a human. After the body dies everything is repeated even though the heart and soul condition will have changed depending on how the soul lived its assigned life. Nevertheless, everything will continue to repeat itself until the true purpose is achieved, which is to return completely to The Creator.

Illustration 15: *True Source Love and Light Brings the Soul into a Mother's Womb*

People often wonder about babies who die when they are still in their mother's womb or only live for a short period of time. They would not have had a chance to learn at all. Usually, in this situation, the soul already knows of the short lifespan prior to agreeing. Usually, the soul does it not for its own learning, but to help those around the soul with their lessons.

B. After Death

Let us now see what happens when someone dies. Although I am using the term 'someone', which we usually use to refer to humans, the explanation I am giving applies to whatever form is used during the incarnation of the spirit.

After death, the temporary physical body of a human returns to the earth *(refer to Illustration 3b:The physical body and consciousness during life and after life)*. However, the non-physical body layers along with the soul, as its center of consciousness, still exist. What will happen to these non-physical body layers and the soul? The answer depends on the condition of the heart. Depending on the condition of the heart, the body layers and the soul may be:

- Carrying Additional Burdens/Attachments
- Brought by the Patrol to a Lower Place for Self-Reflection
- Going to a Better Place
- Souls Brought by Love and Light to Heaven

1. Carrying Additional Burdens/Attachments

The non-physical body layers along with the soul (hereafter referred to just as "soul") may still have attachments for many reasons. Often, the reason that creates this attachment may be something really trivial, but as long as the soul and the heart cannot let it go, the soul will remain attached. The causes of this attachment may be negative emotions towards others or self, busy-ness with personal desires, or attachment to another person or item left behind. Whatever causes the soul, or more accurately the heart, to be unable to let go of those matters, are the causes of the attachments of a soul after death.

These attachments may go on for a very long time. Some of you may have heard of the "ghost" of a lady who has been waiting for her lover to return for decades or even hundreds of years. This can happen because the soul does not have a concept of time. Whatever is overly prioritized by the soul is the one and only concern for the soul.

This is very different for us humans who understand the saying "time is a great healer". This only applies to us who are still alive. While alive, our physical body has a variety of needs such as sleeping, eating, and so forth. Every time we have those needs or engage in related activities, our focus on those attachments will be dispersed little by little. This helps to reduce our excessive attachments.

In the book **The Real You: Beyond Forms and Lives**, I also briefly discussed how our physical need to sleep is actually a very important facility that helps us. We can only have a deep sleep if we let go of all the attachments towards things we are thinking, doing or wanting before we sleep.

Going back to the soul that is still stuck to its burdens/attachments after death, one might question if it will continue like this forever? The answer is no and that it depends on the habits of the soul while still alive. Some souls will be able to let go of their burdens and attachments after some time. This is the moment they will be able to see other things, including passed relatives or officers who come to pick them up and others who will help them to let go of their burdens and attachments (often referred to as angels by those who have experienced a near death experience). Unfortunately, there are also souls who are unable to let go of their burdens and attachments for a very long time. In this situation, there are special officers who are on patrol and will bring them to a lower place for self-reflection.

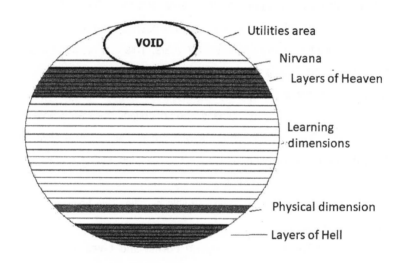

Illustration 16: *The Whole Existence with the Dimmer Dimensions for Self-Reflection Below the Lower Dimensions*

2. The Patrols who Bring Souls to a Lower Place for Self-Reflection

Souls that are unable to let go of their burdens and attachments after some time will be brought by the patrols to a lower, dimmer place. *(Refer to Illustration 16 above)*. Why is this? Even in our dimension, there is an abundance of True Source Love everywhere. Love will always cleanse what is impure or negative, including burdens, attachments, desires and emotions that are within the heart and self of all beings, irrespective of whether that being is alive or has passed away. While still alive, those who do not want to open their heart can easily resist True Source Love by using their physical body as a fortress. However, after death their physical body ceases to exist. Unconsciously, people or souls who are busy with burdens, attachments, desires and emotions will create a dark and thick dome around themselves to limit True Source Love from 'disturbing' their busyness that is consuming them at that very moment *(examine Illustration 17 below)*.

Illustration 17: A Soul that is Busy with
Burdens/Attachments/Emotions Within a Dark Dome

In other words, the soul of someone who has passed away is actually busy with two matters: *firstly*, their emotions and their own desires, and *secondly*, creating and retaining a dark, thick wall so that True Source Love cannot help them. Because of this, the soul needs to be brought to a lower place where True Source Love is not as bright as in this dimension, so the busyness of the soul can be reduced. Meaning that the soul no longer needs to create and retain the wall that blocks True Source Love. In this dimension, the soul can spend time in self-reflection depending on its level of realization

What is meant by self-reflection? A soul that is very busy with its burdens and attachments will usually be consumed with "why is this so, and why is that so?" or "it should have been like this or like that" and so on. If you are perplexed, do not look too far; we are talking about the soul of a human and not an alien from a different planet.

Look at yourself or someone else who is harboring a great desire or strong emotion. When we are still alive, these desires or emotions will be reduced as time passes or by engaging in other activities. However, matters that affect the physical body of a human while alive will no longer affect a soul who has passed away.

The moment the soul is calmer and starts to behave more positively, such as beginning to let go, or wholeheartedly saying, "Let it be...", "It's OK..." or the like, True Source, who has been waiting to help, will be able to help that soul by lifting the soul from this lower place to a place of cleansing/purification. For your information, this lower dimension is not in the first or second dimension, but a special dimension below the first dimension that we often label as hell, which has several layers.

47

3. Going to a Better Place

If an individual is not attached to worldly matters during his or her life and surrenders everything to True Source then, after death, the soul will not have any attachments. In this case, at the point of death, the soul will meet souls of relatives who have also passed and officials that pick them up to be brought to a better place. Souls who previously had light attachments and burdens and are willing to let go of those attachments will also experience this.

However, if we do not open our heart to True Source, then even if that soul is unattached to worldly matters and has given sufficient charity and performed good deeds, the soul will still not be able to recognize the Light and Love that has been given by True Source to bring souls to heaven. So, even though the soul will reach a better place, it will not reach heaven. *(Illustration 18: Arriving in a better place does not mean reaching heaven).*

4. Souls Brought by Love and Light to Heaven

After someone whose heart is quite open and does not have significant attachments and burdens has died, their soul will be able to see the Love and Light that brings souls to heaven, which is different to the tunnel of light that is often mentioned by those who had a near death experience. Often officials who are also bright greet those who experience a near death experience.

This tunnel of light is akin to a *transformer* that takes the soul from our dimension to the other end to True Source Love and Light, beyond all dimensions. This Love and Light is the one that pulls the soul swiftly to be brought upwards (heaven). If you look at **Illustration 19**, you can see how at the end of the tunnel of light there is True Source Love that brings souls into heaven.

Illustration 18: Arriving in a Better Place does not Mean Reaching Heaven

Illustration 19: At the End of the Tunnel of Light is True Source Love that Brings Souls into Heaven

However, even this process can sometimes require quite a long time if, during the process, the soul still has desires, thoughts and does not surrender to True Source.

As True Source Love is unlimited for every being, True Source actually provides that Love and Light for every soul so that every soul can be brought to heaven. Nevertheless, many souls are busy with their burdens and attachments. Even those who do not have attachments are still unable to recognize True Source Love if their hearts are not opened for True Source. Only those with an open heart, free from desires and other matters are able to see and recognize True Source Love. Hence, the key is: **to open our heart to True Source.**

As True Source Love is unlimited for every being, True Source actually provides that Love and Light for every soul so every soul can be brought to heaven.

Chapter 5
Why We Do Not Remember What We Have Experienced In Our Past Lives

We do not remember what we have experienced in our past lives, because in our daily lives, we rely on the memory of the brain that only exists while we are alive. Our current brain didn't exist in previous lifetimes so it is not a matter of actually remembering. We cannot remember because this current brain and physical body never experienced the things that our soul and spirit experienced before our birth in this lifetime.

Our current brain and physical body never experienced the things that we, our soul and spirit, experienced before our birth in this lifetime.

In the *Illustration 20* below, points C and D represent the memory of our brain in this lifetime. Our brain started to exist at Point C. Usually we will remember things we have just experienced, that is closer to Point D. However, we start to forget what we have experienced several months or years ago, because our physical memory is stored in our brain that consists of limited physical cells. In contrast to this, the memory of the soul and the spirit remains intact since they first existed.

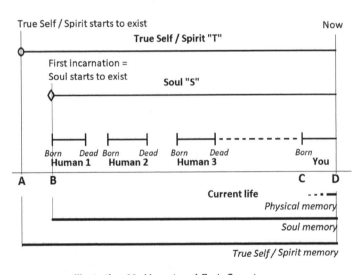

Illustration 20: Memories of Each Consciousness

If you hear stories of people remembering their past lives without using any special practices or methods, then usually, that information is obtained from their higher consciousness, which is their soul consciousness. This is not a common occurrence in humans, because generally speaking, it is not good to remember or to know matters related to our past lives before we are ready. Those who remember involuntarily do so because they require special lessons and therefore need to remember about their past lives.

Many people assume that if we are aware of our past lives and how we have not utilized them properly resulting in our failure to return to True Source completely, then we would be able to improve those weaknesses and complete our lessons in this lifetime. So, why do we not know about our past lives? In general, some of the reasons are:

- We Prioritize our Role More than True Source Love
- We Prioritize what is Important and Interesting to us More than True Source Love
- Our Heart is the Summary of Everything
- All of our Strengths and Weaknesses are Clearly Within us now
- Disturbing Relationships in the Current Life

A. We Prioritize Our Role More than True Source Love

Talking about past lives, many of us will wonder: "Who was I in my past life? Was I a king, a minister, a merchant, a farmer, or...?" When and where did the event happen? This attitude shows how we are too attached to the role that we played in our past lives, while our role is merely the outer layer or facility. The most important part is how we utilized that particular role in order to use our life according to its true purpose.

Irrespective of whether we were a king, commander, minister or even just an ordinary person, all lifetimes and roles give us a chance to use that particular life for True Source Plan, which is to choose True Source completely. Therefore, our role, wherever we were and whenever that lifetime occurred is not important at all.

How are we using our life now? What do we do when beautiful things happen? What do we do when we have problems? What do we do when we have some spare time? What do we do when someone needs our help?

These questions are just some examples and demonstrate our daily attitude, which is intimately related to how we are able to prioritize True Source and True Source Love. We do not need to see this in our past lives because we can recognize it this very moment, in this lifetime.

B. We Prioritize what is Important or Interesting to us More than True Source Love

As well as fixating on the roles we may have had in past lives, we also have a tendency to prioritize what is important and interesting to us rather than what is according to True Source Love. As an example, after I started teaching the "Inner Heart" workshop, participants rarely ask me questions other than those similar to the following:

- "I have been offered a new position, should I accept the new offer or stay where I am now?"
- "I have two choices at work, should I take choice A or choice B?"

Of course we are allowed to use the inner heart for matters we consider important. However, how often do we face those choices? As often as it may be, those choices do not happen every moment in our daily lives. However, True Source is loving us every moment and every moment we experience is a chance to choose True Source more completely. Similar to the previous topic, how much or how often you have used every life experience to prioritize and choose True Source, can be seen in your current life.

C. Our Heart is the Summary of Everything

Whatever role we have been given, however many lifetimes we have experienced, everything is only for the one purpose that still remains unfulfilled. The summary of everything can be seen easily - that is through our heart. Remember that everything is related to our relationship with True Source - to be more precise, how much we would like to choose and prioritize True Source. The condition and attitude of our heart upon our birth reflects all of this.

Illustration 21: A Baby's Heart (The Outermost Layer is Still Clean; Within it, Naughtiness from Past Lives is Stored)

Illustration 22: As the Human Grows up, Naughtiness Starts Seeping Through the Outermost Layer of the Heart and Starts to Influence the Brain

Without needing to remember our roles in past lives, whether we were a king or an ordinary person, without needing to remember whether we lived only for fifty years or more than a hundred years, the way our heart attitude is when we pray to True Source is the summary of all that we have experienced. Not only from previous lifetimes, but since the very beginning.

Illustration 23: The Condition and the Attitude of the Heart in Adulthood if the Heart is not Open

Theoretically speaking, the heart condition at the end of the previous lifetime should be the same as it is now. The only difference is that in every new lifetime, we will acquire a new layer of the heart that also becomes the outermost layer *(refer to Illustration 21).* This is why a newborn baby looks or feels so clean and light. Nevertheless, as time goes by and the baby grows, the naughtiness begins to surface. This naughtiness has been within the spirit ever since the past lifetimes during which it was created. However, it was 'confined' by the clean outer layer of the heart at birth. With time, the naughtiness begins to penetrate the outer layer of the heart and influences the brain of the baby *(See Illustration 22).*

Illustration 24: *The Condition and the Attitude of the Heart at a Late Age if the Heart is not Open*

D. All of our Strengths and Weaknesses are Clearly Within Us Now

In our daily lives, we utilize and recognize mostly our physical consciousness, the brain. Whether we realize it or not, we are not well acquainted with our soul and spirit. Remember that as a human we have three consciousnesses: the brain, soul and spirit. Although we only consciously use our brain, the other consciousnesses, the soul and spirit, still influence us significantly.

This is what I explained previously. The summary of all of our journeys can be seen in the current condition of our heart, for example, how far and wide our heart is opened to True Source or how much our heart surrenders and prioritizes True Source. In relation to our attitude in our daily life, we can recognize within ourselves how clearly we are remembering, choosing and prioritizing True Source. This is what most people fail to understand. Many people assume that learning more about their soul and spirit requires seeking information in faraway places. Yet in fact, the answer is within the depths of each of our own hearts.

How do we differentiate between the reaction of the brain and the reactions of the soul and spirit? Our spirit resides within our heart, so in many ways, our spirit and heart are very close and interrelated. To differentiate, let us examine the following points:

- If it is a thought, analysis or comparison that surfaces, then it originated from our brain
- If it is something that appears spontaneously, then it tends to originate from our soul.
- If it is a feeling that surfaces, then it tends to originate from our heart/spirit.

Often, all three consciousnesses react simultaneously. The one that is expressed would depend on which part we are following. For example, say we are going out of town, how late we are, we see someone fall off their motorbike. Even though we have opened and used our heart, if we are too busy or stressed thinking of how we are already late, we will not be able to sense the feeling or reaction of our heart when we see this event. If we prioritize our own conditions and needs excessively, we may not even care about the person who fell off, and instead justify our actions by assuming that "someone else will help".

The summary of all of our journeys can be seen in the current condition of our heart

If we do not let our busyness and personal desires close our hearts in our daily lives, then in a situation like the example above, where someone is in need of our help, we will be able to feel the reaction of our heart clearly. Love will bloom within our heart for others to help the person who is in need.

Not only will our heart and spirit react, but our soul and brain will as well. Whether or not each consciousnesses would like to help depends on each of their realizations. If you would like to use your life to choose True Source, it is time for you to use every chance to follow the best, which is your heart.

There may be something here that confuses you. In the previous chapters, I mentioned that our naughtiness originated from within our spirit which left True Source, which even refused to be helped directly by True Source. Then, I also said that the spirit is within the heart of every human and the two are very closely connected, in such a way that our feelings originate from our spirit, which is also a reflection of our heart. Yet, in the example above, I said, "Love will bloom within our heart for others to help the person who fell". Aren't these very contradictory?

Without having the complete understanding, you may see these as conflicting ideas. This is why I would like to discuss this specifically so that you can understand the real condition. I hope that you will then be able to understand the relationship between the spirit, the heart and even how to use this life more in accordance with True Source Will.

If we are not using our heart, it is most likely that our spirit is not prioritizing True Source and True Source Will. Our spirit uses all available facilities, including our brain and soul, to fulfill the desires and interests of the spirit. Usually we cannot feel our spirit's influence as we are not using our heart. In these moments, we are too busy with our desires and personal interests that we don't even pay attention to the "whispers" of our own heart, where our spirit resides.

However, if we were using our heart – I say "using our heart" but remember that we cannot do anything to our heart (more details in **Chapter 11**). What really happens is that we let True Source use our heart. When this happens, True Source Love can directly do all the most wonderful things to our heart and our spirit simultaneously. Immediately our spirit will stop its busyness and accept True Source Love directly. We will feel a beautiful feeling in our heart and, at the same time, beautiful and wonderful things are also happening to our spirit.

E. Disturbing Relationships in the Current Life

Another reason why we are not given memories of past lifetimes is because we have different relationships with different souls in each lifetime. As an example, if your child in this lifetime is in fact your enemy from your past life, or your current neighbor was your lover in your past life, then all of these memories will disrupt your thoughts and attitude in this lifetime. You would not be able to act the way you're supposed to.

In my book **Soul Consciousness: An Effective Technique to reach your higher consciousness**, I discuss about the higher consciousness, how to attain it, the purpose and so on. It sounds like this matter is contradictory to what we discussed in this chapter. However, please note that what we discussed in this chapter is aimed at the general public. However, for those who are ready, re-experiencing past lives will be beneficial for their spiritual advancement but this can only be achieved with the proper preparation and method.

Chapter 6
The Real Purpose of Life

Many humans assume that the purpose of their lives is to reach heaven. If you read holy books thoroughly, you will find sentences that state "soul reaches heaven" and many more connections among the soul, heaven and hell. However, in several parts, you will also read sentences related to the "spirit returning to The Creator".

Our brain is a part of the physical body, which is made of flesh and blood. It has limited physical senses, can only feel physical things, and has limited abilities. It is therefore easy to understand why everyone has differing opinions about non-physical matters. To be honest and open, we can see how every person's knowledge is greatly influenced by their background, whether that be culture, beliefs, religion or other significant influences.

Due to our limitation, we blend our background knowledge with the information available to us, and then supplement it with our own assumptions. That is why there is a huge range of different perceptions about non-physical matters. Some people even assume that when a human ceases to exist, everything will disappear without any continuation whatsoever, i.e. no more life. On a whole range of non-physical matters, we may find many similar and conflicting versions and opinions.

It is fair to say generally, to understand these non-physical matters we rely mostly on holy books. Yet, have you ever noticed that the interpretations of the same scripture from a holy book may often vary? Perhaps we have not realized what those holy books are reminding us about; that only our heart can truly realize the true commandment from The Creator.

Let us return to the discussion about the true purpose of human life, which is, in reality, to return to True Source completely. Although we may often hear the expression "returning to True Source" in our daily lives, it is often only used to refer to someone passing away. What I mean by returning to True Source relates to our spirit, or true self. This is the only part of our existence that will continue to exist not only after we die but even until the end of time, when we are together with True Source, according to True Source Will.

The true purpose of a human life is to return to True Source completely

We do not need to die in order for our spirit to return to True Source completely. Most humans have lived numerous times - dozens, hundreds or thousands of times. Still we have not yet achieved the true purpose of life or

Illustration 25: *The Soul Arriving in Heaven is Happy,*
Believing that it has Reached the Real Purpose of Life

the condition necessary to be able to return to True Source. We are not even close. Returning to True Source completely is the purpose of every human's life. Indeed, it has been the purpose of every incarnation of True Source sparks, not only in the current lifetime, but also in every single lifetime that has been experienced and for lifetimes to come. So, returning to True Source is in fact the true purpose of life. It is the reason for each and every lifetime and for the whole of creation.

Why is this so? True Source created the whole earth, every planet, the physical universe and everything else, including heaven and hell, just for the

Ilustration 26: *After Arriving in Heaven, the Soul Remembers that the Final Purpose of Life has not yet been Attained*

sole purpose of providing an opportunity for True Source sparks to have the chance to gain experiences that will help them to choose True Source so that they can be brought back to True Source completely. You can be certain that our non-physical body layers along with the soul, heart, physical body and everything else are also a part of True Source's Grand Plan, which is very beautiful for every one of True Source sparks.

Some spiritual groups say that True Source created us and gave us lives as humans because True Source wanted to acquire our experiences. This is completely untrue. True Source does not need our experiences as True

Ilustration 27: *Even though Heaven is Beautiful, it is only a Temporary Holiday Place – not the Final Destination. Heaven is not the Real Purpose of life*

Source is the All-Knowing. All the life experiences that we have acquired are only there to help us reach one important conclusion - whether on earth or in the afterlife, there is nothing more important or beautiful than True Source Love.

Chapter 7
Various
Spiritual Practices

There are many varied types of spiritual practices because some people consider everything that is non-physical to be a part of spirituality. However, in line with the previous **chapter "The Real Purpose of Life"**, in this chapter, I will limit the review to a few categories of spiritual teaching, such as:

- Special powers/special abilities
- Soul cleansing/soul advancement
- Spirit cleansing/spirit advancement

There are indeed many other spiritual teachings that are beneficial if practiced properly but, because there is such a broad range and there are a limited number of pages in this book, we will limit the discussion to the categorization above.

A. Special Powers/Special Abilities

There are numerous types of spiritual teachings and some may have even become embedded into the culture of local people in different parts of the world. Usually, these spiritual teachings are practices that grant special powers such as self-defense, clairvoyance, the ability to fly, penetrate walls and so on. Some of these abilities sound extraordinary and impossible, but they do exist.

Obtaining unusual abilities is certainly very attractive, irrespective of whether those powers are used to show off or are used when needed for the good of others.

Some people learn these special powers for a simple reason: just to have those special powers. However, there are also those who have obtained special powers as a "side effect" of their endeavors to achieve true spiritual advancement: achieving the true purpose of life, which is to return to True Source completely. Those people may then assume that because of True Source Extraordinary Blessings and by possessing formidable powers, they have a closer relationship with True Source, and that they will have more "access" to various astounding powers and abilities.

B. Soul Cleansing/Soul Advancement

Some people earnestly prioritize the true purpose of life, which is to return to True Source. As it is written in many ancient books that one must dedicate oneself to various methods or special practices, such as yoga for example, people wholeheartedly do those special practices hoping that they will achieve the true purpose of life.

However, many of these practices believe that there is a strong correlation between special abilities or powers and being closer to True Source. In other words, many assume that when someone is closer to True Source, they should have more special abilities.

C. Spirit Cleansing/Spirit Advancement

This discipline is the most rare of them all, because the spirit, or true self, is rarely mentioned in ancient books. In the stories that we read in ancient books, it is often said that:

- Our sprit is our true self
- Our spirit originates from the Creator and is a spark of the Creator
- Only our spirit returns to True Source
- We are only told a little bit about the spirit

In my book **Real You: Beyond Forms and Lives**, I mention a story about a professor in the United States who travelled the world for decades in search of his true self. After many decades, he assumed that he had found his true self, yet what he met was not his true self.

Similarly, one of my late spiritual teachers, who also spent his youth deepening his spiritual understanding, told me that he had achieved his true self consciousness and had reached the true self realm. With what I have personally experienced, I realize that my late teacher actually only reached a higher dimension.

If we read books or articles about our true self, we realize that most of the information is based on concepts, thoughts or what they refer to as *channeling* (receiving messages from spiritual teachers). Actually, if you can use your heart properly, then it becomes very clear how the physical brain cannot understand divine matters. In other words, our limited brain cannot understand the spirit itself.

Please let me remind you again that the spirit of every human and every being is within the heart. Without opening and using the heart, one cannot be connected to the spirit. Then it is just a concept. Without using the heart, it will be impossible for someone to understand his or her spirit, because there are no other parts beyond the heart that can understand anything about the heart or anything within it.

After opening and using the heart, we begin to realize more about why we should not do anything to our spirit. Our heart is a special blessing from True Source as a facility to help our spirit. Whatever happens to our heart will also happen on our spirit. If something positive happens to our heart, our spirit will automatically improve. On the other hand, if something negative happens to our heart, then this negativity will also impact our spirit. This is an important matter that we must know in relation to the meaning of the true afterlife.

D. The Real Benefits from These Three Spiritual Practices

With all due respect to all spiritual practitioners, regardless of the technique that each may practice, I will now discuss the real benefits of the three categories of spiritual teachings mentioned above as they relate to the true purpose of our lives. There are two main themes that we will discuss. *Firstly* let us address whether the related spiritual (non-physical) exercises really are of value to the afterlife or, if they are simply interesting in this temporary life. *Secondly* we will investigate how these exercises relate to the true purpose of life.

Before this, it may be helpful to review our understanding of the term *afterlife* once again. This is important because our perspectives and understandings of the term afterlife may differ. Let us *synchronize* our perspectives and understandings so that we are on the same page for our discussions. This will allow us to understand spirituality more completely.

Many people consider that it is easy to give meaning to the word *afterlife*. It is understood to be something significant to our life whilst on earth and also afterwards. However, let me ask you this question: *which exact afterlife are you referring to?*

If you remember, I mentioned earlier that spiritually speaking, we do not live just once. A being will continuously go through the cycle of life and death until his or her true purpose of life is attained, which is returning to True Source completely. Meanwhile, the word afterlife most commonly refers to the period of time after a lifetime ends.

However, as we live more than once and actually reincarnate again and again until our spirit returns completely to Our Source, The Most Loving Being, then it means that the afterlife is not only experienced after death. The period after death is still a "temporary" period of time because after that, we will be reborn and die again, time and time again until the real purpose is achieved.

That is why, I am clarifying that the term afterlife here does not refer only to an existence after death, instead, it refers to an existence after achieving the true purpose of life. Hence, the common understanding of the term *afterlife* that refers to 'after death' is incorrect. Instead, the true understanding of the afterlife refers to the state of being after achieving the true purpose of life. The true understanding of afterlife is not only something valuable while we are still alive on earth, but it is also beneficial to us in our final place after we have reached the final destiny. So, the understanding of the real afterlife is something that we learn about while on earth. It relates to our true purpose of life, and will guide us to achieve the true purpose of life. Before our first incarnation, we felt that we lacked something and needed something more. That is why True Source, the All Loving and All Caring, gave us this life. Hence, we need to make use of this life in the best way possible to learn about the afterlife for the one true purpose. As this topic is deep and important, we will discuss further in a separate chapter.

The next question is: when we have succeeded in achieving the true afterlife, which is returning to True Source completely, what do we need? Or more accurately, what can we learn while we are still alive on earth, that is valuable to us when we return to True Source completely? Isn't it true that True Source only gives the best? The understanding here is that what's best is not about getting what we need. What's best is always what is given by True Source. This is what we can and need to learn about the afterlife and this understanding will bring us to return to True Source. That is the key.

Now that we understand what we need to know about the true afterlife, it is time to discuss some questions regarding the real benefits of the teachings mentioned at the beginning of this chapter, and the relationship of those teachings with the true purpose of life.

1. Psychic/Special Abilities

Psychic or special abilities are very interesting. How can one not be interested? Imagine if you had abilities that other people didn't have? It would be entertaining, would it not? Some of these abilities include the following:

- Clairvoyance
- Non-physical hearing
- Penetrating walls
- Levitating/flying
- Crushing stones with an empty hand

There are a plethora of these psychic or special abilities. What I have mentioned above are only a few that most people may be familiar with. However, if we look at the list above and consider clairvoyance, non-physical hearing, penetrating walls, levitating/flying and so forth, I would like to ask you all something. After someone dies, can that person do those things?

The answer is "Yes". If we are not busy with our attachments, wants and emotions, we will all be able to see non-physical things, hear non-physical things, penetrate walls, levitate, fly and so forth after we die. Without the physical body, a person's soul, with its non-physical body layers, can for sure see the non-physical things in the same dimension as its non-physical layers. The soul will also be able to hear non-physical things from its dimensions, be able to penetrate walls or other non-physical things, and levitate or fly without being bound by the earth's gravity.

There is one more thing that you forgot. If someone can do all of these things after death, it means that they could do those things even before they were born (or more accurately, before they enter their mother's womb). Knowing this information, what is your opinion now about the question that was asked earlier whether these abilities are of mere worldly interest, or of use to us for the afterlife?

If we are given this life to learn, it is clear that this learning is not about these psychic or special abilities. You may now ask about other abilities or powers that you did not possess before you were born? To answer, let us return to the definition of the afterlife, and to make it easy, ask yourself whether that ability or power will help you to become closer to True Source? If the answer is no, then it is a no.

2. Cleansing/Advancement of the Soul

Cleansing or advancement of the soul is quite a deep discussion. Those who are more committed to pursuing this path generally ignore the psychic or special abilities in order to achieve advancement for their soul. In general, people in this category know that life is temporary; there is only one purpose that is of utmost importance in this life, which is to return to True Source completely.

These people often persevere and go through a variety of practices, including fasting, meditating and many more as a part of the process of cleansing their soul. From these practices, they hope to gradually reach a higher dimension (ascension = ascending to a higher dimension), and then finally achieve the highest dimension, which they believe is the real purpose. However, some may also hope to reach a state of enlightenment, which they believe is the highest spiritual achievement and the true purpose of their lives.

3. Cleansing/Advancement of the Spirit/True Self

As I have mentioned previously, this last category is the least common in the spiritual world due to the lack of information and knowledge about the spirit or true self. There are still many spiritual practitioners who have practiced for years but are still "searching" for their own spirit. From the books that I have read, most people only talk about communicating with their own spirit or even communicating with their own spirit through the mediation of another being whom they assume are angels etc.

At this point, we need to be careful because our desire to attain something quite often makes it easy for us to be fooled by ourselves or other beings. In particular, the ways to communicate with our spirit, either directly or through the help of another being, often give what seems like extraordinary results. Unusual stories that sound incredible to our brain make us busy and we forget the true purpose of life.

There are of course those who speak of ways to be conscious as your spirit. However, most of these methods are also created by the brain and the brain, as we know, has a limited ability to understand our spirit, the spark of Our True Source. A few of those methods created by the brain include consuming special mushrooms, potions or through hypnosis. Are you aware that these methods do not reflect spiritual advancement or a higher consciousness at all?

Why is that? First of all, we need to review the definition of "higher consciousness". It is clearly stated here that a higher consciousness is not the same as the unconscious or subconscious. Those who consume special mushrooms or potions for the sake of experiencing strange sensations will be in a state of unconsciousness or not complete consciousness. What do I mean by consuming special mushrooms or potions? In some cultures or spiritual traditions, by consuming special mushrooms or potions, people experience a trance, which is a state of incomplete consciousness or a subconscious state, and they receive images that they would not receive in their normal daily life. So, that special mushroom or potion is only influencing the person's brain by reducing consciousness and control of the brain, compared to normal daily life. Irrespective of how interesting they are, the visions received are not a real spiritual experience because, in this state they are just hallucinations.

This is similar to undergoing hypnosis. The word hypnosis stems from the word hipnos, referring to the god of sleep in Greek mythology. Hypnosis is a method used in psychology. A psychological dictionary defines hypnosis as a method of communicating with, and to access, the subconscious.

This means that if someone uses hypnosis to attain a higher consciousness, it is in fact not genuine because the subconscious is being accessed and not a higher consciousness at all.

Let us revisit the phrase "higher consciousness". For those of you not familiar with or just becoming acquainted with the term, or indeed those of you who know about higher consciousness but are only familiar with only one or two methods of reaching it, you may perhaps not realize that the term "higher consciousness" already gives us a big clue about what it is about. Bear with me while I elaborate further. I have explored many matters related to higher consciousnesses for dozens of years. I have travelled the world, teaching, meeting, discussing and practicing with people from all kinds of backgrounds. Many of them are professionals in their field, including medical doctors, psychology professors and yoga practitioners from India. Every year, people from many countries including India, United States, Canada, New Zealand, Ireland, England, Germany come to learn and directly experience what it is to shift to higher consciousnesses including to their own true self consciousness.

I have helped thousands of people to reach their higher consciousness, whether it be their soul and/or their spirit/true self. One of the most important matters related to our higher consciousness is that when we are in a higher consciousness, we are still in a completely conscious state. So, our consciousness remains completely undisturbed. We can still remember our name, address and etc. and we are also fully conscious of what we are doing, where we are, and so forth.

It is called experiencing a "higher consciousness" because other than our normal daily consciousness, we simultaneously experience a different, higher, consciousness of our own. If it is not our own consciousness it means we are being possessed.

Being in a higher consciousness is completely different to being possessed. Being possessed means that there is a different consciousness within a person's self that is influencing or even controlling the consciousness of the person being possessed.

To help you understand the previous statement, you can refer to the illustration below.

Please ensure that you remember the final and true purpose. Without remembering the final and true purpose, we may take the wrong path in this deep journey. If your final purpose is to return to True Source completely and you are already heading in the right direction, you are for

Illustration 28: *A Possessed Soul Being Influenced by Another Being's Consciousness Within Him/Her*

sure already closer to True Source. You should be able to surrender more to True Source and be grateful more often to True Source. Additionally, don't forget the important matter of the key to our connection with True Source, which is our heart. You should also have already opened your heart more completely to True Source.

If you feel that your practices have advanced you in the cleansing and development of your spirit/true self but you do not feel closer to True Source, then something is definitely not right. The journey of our spirit is only to be closer to True Source. Please be careful with the terminology "feeling closer to True Source". Remember that in spirituality, we are our own biggest enemy. As we often trick and deceive ourselves in our everyday lives, we also often fool ourselves in feeling that we are "closer to True Source".

How can we be aware if we are being fooled or not? If "feeling closer to True Source" is followed by feelings of "pride", "sense of cleverness", and so on, then it is clear that you are being fooled. Being closer to True Source should naturally be followed by humbleness, gratitude to True Source, loving others, patience, calmness, peacefulness and so on. We will remember and long for True Source more frequently in every matter. We will also be more wholehearted and humble, remembering True Source, living our life as an offering of love for True Source.

So, if we may return to the topic of our discussion about the cleansing and development of our spirit/true self, even though this is a good thing, it is still quite a rare occurrence for spiritual practitioners to achieve this through their practices. This is why I am writing this book and many other books in the hope that I may be able to give a little insight so that more people can realize the true purpose of life and to do the best according to that purpose.

Chapter 8
Common Concepts
vs. The Real
Spiritual Journey

To give you more information, first we will discuss common concepts related to the spiritual journey, how to achieve it and so forth. Then, we will look at the real journey and the ways to attain it.

A. Common Concepts of the Spiritual Journey

Right now we are on earth. Some people know that we have a special purpose, a purpose that cannot be found on this earth but something that makes us better and purer. These people often have a tendency to assume that reaching their destiny is reaching the highest place in the whole existence. To achieve this, they do various things to cleanse and purify their self in order to continuously ascend to higher places with the hope that, one day, they reach the highest place. The concept of continuously ascending to higher places is often referred to as *ascension*.

For those of you who are interested and would like to try the *ascension* method, I must remind you that there are 365 levels of learning dimensions. As our earth is the third dimension, another 362 dimensions still remain above our earth. If you would like to implement this method, you would have to ascend 362 dimensions just to reach the highest learning dimension.[2] Beyond the highest learning dimension, there are still higher places, which are the layers of heaven.

Nevertheless, there is no intelligence or power that can bring you to heaven, other than True Source Love. You may recall from our previous discussions, even if your soul can enter heaven, you will still need to be reborn.

We have also often heard that if our soul attains perfect enlightenment, where everything impure (negative karma) within us dissolves, then our soul will reach the highest place. This highest place is often referred to as Nirvana. Nirvana is a place even higher than the highest heaven. Souls in nirvana do not need to be reborn. Is nirvana our true destiny? Isn't it true that we do not need to be reborn if we have reached Nirvana? Does reaching Nirvana mean that our "duties" are also completed?

The answer to these questions is: No. Nirvana is not the true destiny. We only have one destiny: to return to True Source completely. Nirvana is only referred to as a place which is higher than the highest heaven, not as a place where the spirit can return to True Source. Many people also assume that True Source is in the highest place. However, as we have previously discussed, divine matters are separated from ordinary non-physical matters. For sure True Source, the Source of Everything is not simply in the highest

---

[2] We do not discuss about the lower dimensions where the first and second dimensions are located because in one's spiritual journey, one does not want to travel to a lower dimension, other than to accumulate power. The spiritual journey is related to attaining a higher place/dimension.

non-physical place, but in a very special place that cannot be accessed by anyone's soul. Only our spirit, the spark of True Source can return completely to True Source.

You may be asking, isn't the soul of those who have reached nirvana free from all karma? Yes, however there is one related matter that I will reveal that many of you may not believe. Notwithstanding this, what I am sharing with you is the real truth. True Source is the All Loving. When we received our soul from True Source for the very first time, our soul was in a pure, perfect condition, free of any karma. Hence, if you only cleanse and purify the soul or just your negative karma, it means you are simply returning to square one. Cleansing the soul and the karma from our own wrongdoings means that we have changed and we no longer follow and choose our wants. But the true purpose of our lives, the true purpose of all of our journeys, will not yet have been achieved.

Although the naughtiness of the spirit is no longer explosive, because we have not followed it for quite some time, the naughtiness and weakness of our spirit still exists within our spirit. Only True Source Love can cleanse those weaknesses and this can only happen through our heart. Additionally, please remember that even if the naughtiness and weaknesses of the spirit are completely gone, if our spirit has not chosen and prioritized True Source then our spirit will not have accepted the most beautiful Gift of Love from True Source, to bring us to return to True Source.

B. The Real Spiritual Journey

As we are now discussing our journey, we shall begin with points that are pertinent to embarking on this journey. What are the most important things that we must have or know before we embark on the journey? We will need to at least have, or know:

- The Map/Direction, to clearly know the goal and the direction
- Vehicle/Facilities that we need for that particular journey. For example if our destination is across the ocean, then we will need a plane or a ship. Even the best land vehicle will not be able to bring us across the ocean.
- Other relevant matters

Let us discuss the above points one by one:

1. The Map/Direction

I have previously mentioned that the highest dimension, even nirvana, which is beyond all dimensions, is not the real destiny. So, where is our true destiny? To know the real destiny, we need to return to ***Illustration 16: The whole existence with the dimmer dimensions below the first dimension for self-reflection.*** In that illustration, you can see the 365 learning dimensions, with the planning dimension, layers of heaven and nirvana as the highest place above it. However, there is something higher than nirvana that is unknown to the soul. In our limited human language, we refer to this as the *spirit realm,* also referred to as the void, as nothing other than spirits exists there. This is where every spirit exists, including the spirit of The Creator. This is our true destiny which is rarely known by people as this place cannot be seen or reached by any other form or level of consciousness other than the spirit.

Another important fact that you should know is that the spirit of every human and every being is within the void. This moment, every moment, long before you and I were born and even beyond our deaths, our spirits will always be in the void. The spirit in the void is our main spirit. The spirit within your body on earth at this moment, is only a small part of your real spirit (for further information, please refer to the book **Real You: Beyond Forms and Lives**.)

Related to the void, there is actually something more important than nirvana and all layers of heaven. In **Chapter 6: The True Purpose of Life**, we discussed that "the soul enters heaven", meanwhile "the spirit returns to True Source".

In other words, the journey of the spirit or the true purpose of our life is not related to a particular place we are heading towards, but relates to our connection with True Source, which is to choose and prioritize True Source. If we accept the Blessings to be brought to return to True Source, to be with True Source, we will for sure be in the most beautiful, best and highest place. The place is just a "side effect" of being together with True Source.

Up to here, can you see how important it is to have awareness about these matters, including having a clear map and direction? Without realizing these matters, someone may try very hard to bring him or herself from earth to ascend through hundreds of dimensions. This would be extremely challenging – or even impossible. The most important matter to realize is that even in attaining the highest place, even nirvana, we have not yet achieved the true purpose of life.

In **Illustration 29**, you can see how some spirits are closer to the Creator while others are further away. Returning completely to True Source means our spirit is wholeheartedly prioritizing True Source, is not separated from True Source, and becomes a part of the Love and Light completely.

The journey of the spirit is not about reaching a place; rather, it is about our relationship with True Source, how we choose and prioritize True Source

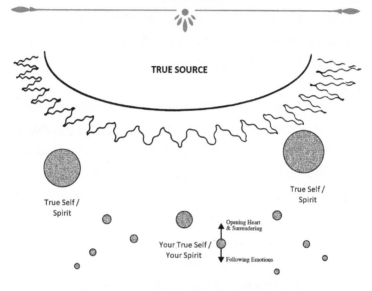

Illustration 29: *All Spirits Before True Source in the Spirit World (Those Closer to True Source are Brighter and Bigger; those Further away are Smaller and Dimmer)*

To avoid misunderstanding, returning to True Source completely does not mean that we become equal with the Creator. That would be impossible. We are just a speck of dust and cannot do anything. We exist and our existence is meaningful only because of the unlimited Love of True Source for us. Returning to True Source completely in our limited worldly language can be likened to a speck of dust that sticks to the sole of the feet of The Creator. We will always be insignificant specks of dust but we will no longer be separated from True Source. This is eternal true joy where our spirit can be a part of True Source Love and Light completely.

If you have realized what has been discussed up to this point, you should already have understood a couple of important matters: Firstly, forget about trying to reach any dimension, because since before time started, our spirit has always been in the void. Secondly, whichever dimension we reach does not have any positive effect on our spirit at all. On the other hand, our busyness in trying to achieve a different or higher dimension may even take our spirit further away from True Source. Our true journey is not related to any dimensions or our soul reaching any dimension. Not at all. On the contrary, it is to choose and prioritize True Source, the All Loving.

2. Vehicle/Facilities

After discussing the direction (the true purpose of life), the next question that arises is how we attain that purpose. In order to achieve the true purpose, we will definitely need some kind of vehicle or facility. We already know that the true purpose is completely unrelated to a place or any dimension. Since the very beginning, our spirits have always existed in the void. The true purpose is to become as close as possible to True Source. Therefore, we ask, which method will bring us to be as close as possible to True Source?

Spirits that are closer to True Source in the spirit world are brighter and bigger, while those further away are smaller and dimmer.

Please understand that there are no techniques, powers, or methods that will be able to bring us closer to True Source, other than True Source Love. All beings are subjects of True Source. There is no one and no thing that can be compared to True Source. No beings, including the holiest or the highest, can bring us closer to True Source other than True Source or, more specifically, True Source Love. The only thing that we can do is to open our hearts to True Source, surrendering ourselves with humbleness to choose and prioritize True Source.

3. Other Relevant Matters

To clarify, there are no techniques, intelligences, powers or any other matters at all that will be able to help us be closer to True Source, which is the true purpose of our lives. All this time, it was our spirits who rejected the Love because we prioritized other matters. True Source never left us. Our spirits were the ones who left True Source, yet True Source Unlimited Love wants to bring us to return to True Source. So all we need to do is to "remind" our spirit to surrender all of its desires and interests and choose True Source continuously until our spirit can choose and prioritize True Source completely.

By comparing the generally accepted concept of a spiritual journey to the real spiritual journey, we can see that most people's perception is very different to the real spiritual journey. For the best result, it is not appropriate to mix the generally accepted perceptions of the spiritual journey and purpose with the real spiritual journey. Moreover, the generally accepted concepts that the public may be familiar with are not a stepping-stone to the real journey. In reality, the direction and purpose of the two are very different. Nonetheless, to those who are none the wiser, the two may appear somewhat similar.

Chapter 9
Keys of Basic Realizations

The true spiritual journey, which is the true purpose of our lives, is a deep subject. Even though I have explained a lot, so that you do not forget, I will repeat several important keys to emphasize the most basic matters that many people do not understand. Without proper understanding of these matters, even those who would like to use their lives as a facility to choose and prioritize True Source completely may take the wrong step, because they assume that the step they take is one of many or even the one and only choice to reach the true purpose of life.

Those who I meet often say that there is more than one way to achieve the true purpose of life, spiritually speaking. I understand that many of you have carried various concepts for many years that are based on each of your different backgrounds. Hence, it is very important to understand and realize at a deep level every one of these insights given below in order to let go of the concepts that have been entrenched within us for many years.

At the very least, we need to clearly know and understand the following matters:

- The true purpose of life is not about reaching a place
- The deepest consciousness
- The condition of the soul before the very first incarnation
- Incarnation (life) is a beautiful gift from True Source
- The true purpose is to return to True Source
- Nobody can help us to be closer to True Source other than True Source
- The reason why only True Source Love can bring our spirit closer to True Source

By discussing these important matters separately and from a slightly different point of view, I hope that you will understand and have deeper realizations about each of these matters. Only after you have properly appreciated and understood the matters mentioned above will you be able to realize the "true way". After that we will be able to discuss "the true way" more easily.

A. The True Purpose of Life is not About Reaching a Place

The true purpose of life is not a place. For so long, many people have assumed that the true purpose of a human's life is to reach the best or highest place. So many humans believe that reaching a better place is the true purpose and the direction of life. Therefore, it is crucial to realize that our true purpose of life is not about reaching even the most special place. Even though heaven really does exist up there above all the learning dimensions, our true goal is not heaven; it is unrelated to a place. If we assume that returning to True Source means that we need to go to a specific place where True Source resides, then we will tend to rely on our ways and abilities or ask for help from different beings to attain it.

The highest place that we can possibly achieve with our ability or with the help of other beings is only the highest learning dimension, which is the 365th dimension, a dimension, or place, where we will meet other beings that are also still learning. With our own abilities or with the help of other beings, we cannot even reach the lowest level of heaven. Only True Source Love can bring us beyond the border of the highest learning dimension to reach places higher than the 365th dimension.

So, it is vital for us to realize that our true goal is not a place; rather, it is about our relationship with True Source. It is about being able to prioritize True Source completely. At the same time we will be able to accept True Source Gift of Love to bring us to return to True Source completely. And accordingly, we will remain with True Source forever.

B. The Deepest Consciousness

We have many layers of consciousness. The deepest consciousness is our spirit/true self that is the spark of True Source. Many spiritual practitioners have likened the many layers of human consciousness to the layers of an onion. If you are already aware of this, then do not seek to peel back just a part of the layer, but peel off everything to completion, to reach the truest consciousness, which is the spark of True Source that resides within us.

Do not peel back just a part of the layer, but peel off everything to completion, to reach the truest consciousness, which is the spark of True Source that resides within us

In practice, those who attempt to do so will encounter a problem. Even those who really dedicate themselves to completely peeling off every layer within themselves, will not be able to do so as our true consciousness resides within the heart. The heart is very special, and we cannot do anything to our own heart. Since we cannot do anything to our heart, we cannot reach the true consciousness within our heart through our own efforts. Without opening their heart properly, many spiritual practitioners who have spent decades practicing or following thousands of years of tradition are still not able to reach the deepest consciousness. The deepest consciousness is the true consciousness otherwise known as our spirit.

The heart is very special,
and we cannot do anything to our own heart.

C. The Condition of the Soul Before the Very First Incarnation

In relation to the previous topic of our many layers of consciousness, our soul consciousness is not our true consciousness, although it is one of the consciousnesses within us. Many people who are on a spiritual journey are only dedicated to cleansing their soul or cleansing their negative karma (it is usually the combination of both). What they have forgotten, or are unaware of, is the reason that we were given a soul in the first place. Recognizing this reason is very important to the spiritual journey and to attaining our true purpose.

Cleansing or purifying our soul will not enable us to achieve our real purpose. This fact will be especially clear when we remember again the journey we have travelled since before we were given a soul. We need to realize that our soul did not just come into existence on its own accord. Our soul is a gift of Love from the Creator. Our soul was pure and perfect the very first time it was gifted to us by the Creator, beyond the purity and perfection of any soul we know of now. Moreover, our soul did not have any karma at all the very first moment it was given to us. Why? The answer is very easy: because we had not yet done anything. As karma is the result of actions, without any actions, there would not yet be any karma.

So, karma is only the side effect of the journey we have been through. Erasing negative karma is also not the true purpose of our lives. In a manner of speaking, reaching the most beautiful and best place in the existence is similar to erasing negative karma and having a purified soul as both are only the "side effects" of returning to True Source completely. As True Source is the one and only Source of All that is the most beautiful, it follows that the most beautiful and perfect things can only be given by True Source, not from any kind of personal effort, nor from the help of anyone else.

Our soul was pure and perfect the very first moment it was gifted to us by the Creator, way beyond the purity and perfection of any soul we know of now.

I am fully aware that what I just stated will certainly create disagreements from many parties because it is contradictory to what many have learnt and believed for a long time. However, what I have expressed is not merely my own personal ideas; rather it is what I have realized after personally remembering and re-experiencing everything my spirit has experienced since the very beginning. And kindly listen to what your own heart says in relation to everything we are discussing. It is time for you to trust your heart more rather than just relying on what your brain hears or reads. If any part of this book has created disagreements within your mind, then re-read that part and pay attention to how your heart reacts as you read it, realizing what your heart knows.

Another interesting topic that I would like to address is how profound spiritual matters are realized at a deep level. Our brain is not able to reach a deep level of realization on profound spiritual matters. Our brain will try to guess or speculate and usually, because of our limitations, the speculation will be incorrect. Only our heart has the ability to realize very deep spiritual matters. After we realize something with our heart, our brain will also be able to recognize that our previously incorrect concepts contradict other facts, in other words, they are illogical. All truths from the heart are highly interrelated and support one another. None are contradictory, because this is how the truth should be.

In relation to how the truth should be logical, I mentioned previously one example relating to the time before our soul existed. Our soul had not yet committed any actions and therefore could not have acquired any karma at all. Likewise, as a spirit, we did not interact with the universe or the whole existence, so we did not create any karma then either.

Moreover, because our souls are the most beautiful Gifts of Love from True Source, it is time we realize more about the meaning of saying "True Source the Almighty and the All Loving". We realize for sure that True Source gives us the best. After all, True Source is the All Loving. This is the truth. However, all beings, including us, who are still within the learning dimensions are not yet perfect and are seeking perfection. Who are we then to think that, as imperfect beings, we would be able to realize the true meaning of perfection and that we would be able to reach perfection?

Your heart knows the clear answer to the above questions. Everything will become clearer, especially, if you trust your heart and inner heart[3] more.

Let us return to the topic of achieving our true purpose. In the process of achieving the true purpose, you will still need to go through cleansing of the soul and do good deeds. However, the purpose is neither to perfect your soul nor to erase negative karma. Those things are just a part of achieving the true purpose.

---

[3] Our Heart is the center of our feeling, where our spirit resides. Our Heart is also very special, because it cannot be influenced by other beings no matter how advanced they may be. Only we can dirty our own heart and only True Source can cleanse, open and do the best things to our heart. For that reason, our heart knows the truth because it is not influenced by other matters/beings. Furthermore, we also have the Inner Heart, which is the core of our Heart and also the core of our Spirit, the real spark of True Source. As the deepest core of our Heart, our Inner Heart also knows truths much better than our Heart, because the Inner Heart is the purest part of our Heart.

D. Incarnation (Life): A Beautiful Blessing from True Source

Referring back to our previous topics, many people are starting to realize that we have lived thousands of lifetimes and therefore we should begin using this life wholeheartedly for the true purpose, rather than being busy with our wants and other worldly matters. Nevertheless, without realizing the initial cause of this journey (incarnation & reincarnation), many will perceive this cycle of reincarnation as a suffering. I would like to say that this opinion is incorrect.

Let us reflect on our true selves who actually needs True Source but left True Source. As True Source is the All Loving, True Source helps us in abundant ways to bring us closer to True Source. However, despite this our spirits are still rejecting True Source. Our lives that repeat over and over again are the beautiful recurring opportunities, given by True Source, for us to experience different lifetimes so that we can remember True Source and be willing to be helped by True Source to return completely to True Source.

If we truly understand all of this, we can realize that life and incarnation is not a suffering, but rather, a beautiful Gift of Love from True Source. Not using our lives in accordance to True Source Plan/Will, and being preoccupied with our busyness and desires is the real suffering. It is easy to mix up these two understandings, though in reality, they are very different. Our realization about this matter also influences our attitude. If you are able to clearly feel with your heart, try to feel your heart attitude with the following realizations:

1. Life is a suffering, which is why we need to do our best to reach the true purpose of life.
2. Life is a beautiful Gift of Love from True Source that we must use properly to reach the true purpose of life.

Life/Incarnation is not a suffering,
It is a beautiful Gift of Love from True Source

If you can feel the differences, it will be very clear that the first attitude will fuel our desires. We will struggle to do things and exert effort to achieve the purpose of our lives, which then actually just comes from our own endeavors. Even though we may pray to True Source, our heart attitude will still be limited. In a sense, we are only using True Source to reach our goals.

In contrast, with the second attitude, you will be able to feel beautiful feelings, such as gratitude to True Source. Our heart will be filled with gratitude to True Source. We will live our lives and use all the beautiful facilities given by True Source in our gratitude to True Source and automatically our attitude to True Source will be different in every matter.

E. The True Purpose is to Return to True Source

Although I have mentioned this numerous times in my book, I still feel the need to repeat this again in this chapter. Our true purpose is to return to True Source. Many people assume that they already know this, but it is time for you to understand more deeply about the following matters. Ask yourself:

- Will the spiritual practices you are doing bring you closer to True Source?
- Are you remembering, trusting and surrendering more and more to True Source in your thoughts, feelings and actions?
- Are you becoming more grateful to True Source?

- Are you being more grateful for everything you go through in your daily life?
- Are you judging others less and less?
- Are you loving and caring for others more and more?
- Do you feel lighter and more joyful in your daily life?

If you answer "no" even for only one of the questions above, it means that there is still something missing. If what you do is really bringing you closer to True Source, then you realize that all of the above are only indicators of being closer to True Source. This is because our true purpose is about our relationship with True Source, to choose and prioritize True Source by surrendering our desires and interests to True Source. If you have applied the teachings properly, then the above points will happen automatically in your daily life.

F. Nobody can Help us to be Closer to True Source Other than True Source

Remember that we may have a direct relationship with True Source without any intermediaries because we are gifted with the special privilege of communicating directly with True Source.

Even in our journey to be closer to True Source, we cannot be mediated by anyone at all. This does not mean that for us to communicate directly with True Source we have to hide in caves on the top of mountains so we do not interact with other beings. Humans are created as social beings. In interacting with others, we learn to love one another, we learn to surrender our desires, and we learn that we cannot live without others.

However, spiritually speaking, all help from others is there to remind us about our true purpose of life, to trust and surrender to True Source from our hearts. In our relationship with True Source, everything must be done directly. So, nothing other than True Source Love can help us to be closer to True Source - not a spiritual teacher, a holy being, an angel or any other being. Other beings are all subjects of True Source, the same as us. In directing ourselves to return to True Source, other beings can only help by reminding us of our true purpose. We are the ones who must consciously choose True Source and True Source Love. These choices are the ones that will make our heart prioritize True Source more and accept True Source unlimited Love for us, to become closer to True Source.

It is only when we face the situation where the desires from within us surfaces, by being helped by True Source Love, the same causes that made our spirit leave True Source, can be eliminated. This process may need repeating tens of times, maybe even more. Nevertheless, in each and every one of those instances, True Source Love can help us. When our bad habits (such as smoking) disappears, without realizing, we have let True Source Love help us a reasonable amount in diminishing the things within our spirit that cause us to not prioritize True Source the All Loving.

As a bad habit disappears, it does not mean that all negative matters in our spirit are gone. However, it means that we are several steps closer to True Source. Remember that complete changes can only happen to our spirit when True Source Love helps us through our heart. Without the help of True Source Love, we are only preventing the impulses from reaching the surface. However, it does not mean that you may not receive help from other facilities or people in getting rid of your bad habits. We may receive help and we can use other facilities, as long as it does not involve other beings' power to change ourselves. If that is the case, we are being programmed or remain under the influence of those powers.

G. The Reason why only True Source Love can Bring our Spirits to be Closer to True Source

I would like to add several further important points in relation to why only True Source Love can help us to be closer to True Source, especially in bringing us to return completely to True Source. The consciousness that we are familiar with in our daily lives is our physical mind. Many people practice various spiritual techniques, whether by meditating or living as ascetics, to advance their soul. Even though the journey of returning to True Source completely is the journey of the spirit, not the soul and certainly not the physical body. The spirit within our heart is only a small part of the main spirit – the main spirit is within the void.

Please remember that the heart and spirit are very special. We cannot do anything to them even though our heart and spirit are "our own". This is because the heart and spirit are beyond all dimensions and that's the way they naturally are. If we were adamant in doing something to our heart and spirit, the result would be catastrophic. Only True Source Love can do the most beautiful and wonderful things, we only need to let all the most beautiful and wonderful things happen (by surrendering to True Source).

Next, I will also describe to you about the naughtiness and weaknesses within our spirit and its relationship with our heart and lives. This explanation is actually a continuation of the previous story of the heart of a newborn baby. If you recall, a child has the same heart at birth as they did when they passed away in their previous lifetime. The difference is that in this new lifetime, the baby receives a clean outermost layer for his or her heart.

The naughtiness within the spirit will try to influence the soul and brain. Usually, after a few years, the naughtiness from the spirit will start to penetrate the outermost layer of the heart that started off clean and it will begin to influence the soul and brain. This becomes visible by the behavior

100

of the baby who is now a toddler. The naughtiness from the spirit will continue to penetrate the new outermost layer of the heart until it can dominate the whole outermost layer, the soul and the spirit.

The naughtiness from the spirit (that is already within the heart), will not be able to come out if the toddler's behavior is disciplined by parents or his/her upbringing is influeneced by positive guidance from the environment. Moreover, self-discipline as an adult through personal realizations, and by not following the impulses from the naughtiness within, will also prevent the naughtiness from coming out. Maintaining a clean self and continuously not following the impulses of the naughtiness will make the soul and brain steadily cleaner and brighter. However, it will still not be able to cleanse the negativities within the heart.

Only by relying on True Source Love that can instantly do the most beautiful things, can the cleansing happen to the brain, soul, every layer of the heart, the spirit, and even to the deepest cause within the spirit. I am referring to the same causes that made our spirit leave True Source and the same things that still hinder us from accepting the most beautiful Gift of Love from True Source. To bring us to return completely to True Source.

Even though I say that True Source Love can instantly do all the most beautiful things, it does not mean that everything will be taken care of in an instant. Even walking towards the door requires taking several steps. The most important part is having a clear and correct direction and to continue stepping forward until we reach the door. Similar to this analogy, if we already know and realize our true purpose of life and how True Source Love is the best, we can use every moment of our lives to let True Source Love help our spirit and us. I will discuss everything in more detail so that the attitude of our whole heart and self can develop to the best state to be helped by True Source Love.

Up to here, the most important points to remember and realize are that the true purpose of our lives is to return to True Source completely and that the main cause of leaving True Source was prioritizing our desires over True Source. Therefore, choosing True Source at every step and using every moment to this end is a vital key in choosing and prioritizing True Source completely. After all, how can we claim to prioritize True Source if we are still relying on ourselves or other powers? Relying on ourselves or other powers simply shows that we do not yet trust True Source completely and we are not yet willing to rely on True Source Love completely.

Chapter 10
The Real Path

It should be clear from all the discussions so far that the true purpose of life is to return to True Source. Only True Source Love can bring us to return to True Source completely and to be even closer to True Source. No other being can help us other than True Source.

True Source Love, as the one and only way to be closer and to return to True Source, is absolute. It cannot be mixed with anything else. Unlike choosing food, where we can pick two types of dishes at once, there is only one way to return to True Source completely, which is True Source Love.

True Source, the Creator, is the Source of every human spirit, irrespective of their background and including those who do not believe in True Source. Therefore, the way to return to True Source completely certainly does not belong to a specific group of people. On the contrary, it is the Will of True Source for every being to use the way provided and that includes all humans.

True Source Love is given to all humans and all beings in order to bring every one of True Source sparks to return completely. However, it is just not enough for us to merely think about or want to accept the Love. We must use the way that has been provided by True Source according to True Source Will.

In order to use the beautiful way that has been provided by True Source personally, there are several important keys that must be realized and put into action. These are:

- First Key: Using the Heart
- Second Key: Using the Inner Heart
- Third Key: Trusting True Source completely
- Fourth Key: The direction is to be loved by True Source
- Fifth Key: Surrendering to True Source
- Sixth Key: Using every moment in life to choose True Source
- Seventh Key: Being grateful every moment to True Source
- Eighth Key: Sharing True Source Love with all beings

Although in this explanation I share the important keys in eight categories or stages, there is nothing special about the actual number eight. I simply categorized it to ease our discussion. Depending on the perspective or level of discussion, I often categorize the discussion topics in different ways.

Some of you may question why trusting True Source completely, which is something very important in our relationship with True Source, is placed as the third key and not the first key? The reason is that in this context, I am not speaking of trusting True Source in just a general sense. The kind of trust in True Source that I am referring to is a deeper trust to reach the true purpose of life.

A. The First Key: Using Our Heart

The first key, which is the most important in using the way that has been provided by True Source personally, is **opening and using our hearts**. As discussed in **Chapter 3,** in the section about the Relationship between the Spirit and the Heart, this physical life and our human bodies are Gifts of Love from True Source. True Source personally gave us these gifts to help our spirits, who left True Source and did not want to be helped, to return to True Source. Through experiencing life using this physical body and brain, we can realize how limited and temporary everything is. Only True Source and True Source Love are eternal. We should therefore remember True Source, remember True Source Love, and remember who we really are, which is the spirit, the **"sparks"** of True Source. We should also remember that we left True Source, and we need True Source Help to let us return completely to True Source, according to True Source Will. With this understanding, we can realize better how to use our lives in the best way possible as a facility according to True Source Plan. That means using our lives as a facility to choose True Source, surrendering our desires and prioritizing True Source the Almighty more and more.

At this point, don't let yourself be fooled by your own mind. Even though your mind is willing to prioritize True Source, it is the words of a brain that only exists temporarily. To reach the true purpose, we need our spirit to say "yes" to choose and prioritize True Source, the Most Holy. This is why we need to use our heart, which is the key connection between us as a whole, and True Source. Our heart is also the key between our brain and our spirit. Only when we pray to True Source using the heart can our spirit also pray to True Source at the same time. Only at the moment when our brain surrenders its interests and chooses to pray to True Source, and when it surrenders more to True Source, can the same thing also happen to our spirit. But this can only happen if we do so using our heart. Consequently, step-by-step, what we go through in life can continuously improve our relationship as a whole (including our spirit) with True Source, who is our only Source and our only Destiny.

B. The Second Key: Using Our Inner Heart

Our heart is often referred to as the key connection between True Source and us. By using our heart when we are praying and communicating to True Source, will our spirit also pray and communicate with True Source. As a result, the relationship between our whole self and our spirit with True Source will improve. However, only using the heart is not enough when talking about the true purpose of life, which is to return to True Source completely. We must also use the Inner Heart. Only then can we use our heart and open our heart to True Source completely.

The Inner Heart is the core of our heart. Without using the Inner Heart, our heart will not be able to open completely to True Source. The Inner Heart is also important in our spiritual journey to help us avoid taking the wrong step, because only the Inner Heart can truly realize True Source Will.

C. The Third Key: Trusting True Source Completely

As I have previously mentioned, using the heart in our relationship with True Source is not enough. We must also trust True Source, but not the kind of trust where we are only paying lip service. We need to trust that True Source really loves and cares for us completely, trusting that True Source wants to help and guide us every moment and will bring us to return completely to True Source.

Many of us say that we trust True Source completely. Yet look at the reality. Often in life we are dissatisfied or disappointed in True Source. We also often follow True Source Will only because of fear of punishment. So, our trust in True Source is still wavering or very limited. We do not yet totally trust that True Source loves us completely. This is a significant matter. If we do not yet fully trust that True Source loves us completely, how can we rely on True Source Love completely?

I would like to emphasize again that trusting True Source is not simply lip service. We must trust True Source completely. However, only after we open and use our heart and Inner Heart can we trust True Source better. After opening and using the Inner Heart properly, especially if we are trusting True Source completely, can we clearly feel how bizarre it is to think that True Source is, or has ever been, angry at us. Our Heart and Inner Heart knows the real truth.

So, we need to have absolute trust in True Source and trusting does take time. After our heart is opened and we personally experience beautiful things in our relationship with True Source, then our trust in True Source will improve continuously until we can trust True Source completely.

If we do not yet fully trust that True Source loves us completely, how could we rely on True Source Love completely?

D. The Fourth Key: The Direction is to be Loved and Taken Care of by True Source

Our relationship with True Source is very deep. True Source Will is for our relationship with True Source to be more than mere courtesy, not just to be closer, but to really help our spirit, which left True Source, to return completely to True Source. After trusting True Source, the next stage is to do everything only to be loved by True Source. Without following this course, even though we are doing things that are according to True Source Will, due to our weaknesses we will still expect something in return. So, unconsciously we are following True Source Will for our own interests. Only if we do everything just to follow the course of being loved by True Source, can our various weaknesses automatically diminish, including our lack of sincerity.

E. The Fifth Key: Surrendering to True Source

Surrendering to True Source is something that is often talked about but not easily done. Similar to trusting True Source completely, the heart and Inner Heart are the initial keys. We must already be using the heart and Inner Heart properly, otherwise surrendering will be a mere concept from our mind. Other than that, we must also have sufficient trust in True Source. Without trusting True Source sufficiently, how can we surrender to True Source? For example, if we do not trust that True Source loves us completely and that True Source really does want to give us the best, including bringing us to return completely to True Source, we may busy ourselves with all kinds of endeavors with the intention of getting closer to True Source. In doing these various things, we have the tendency to expect something in return, essentially related to gaining profit for ourselves.

On the other hand, when we really trust True Source, that True Source really loves us completely, and that True Source really wants to give us the best, including bringing us to return completely to True Source, only then can we surrender to True Source. This important realization brings us great relief as we understand that this tremendously important and significant matter to return to True Source is not a "duty" for us to uphold. Instead, it is a "A beautiful Gift of Love from True Source" for us to accept. This realization will make our attitude very different. We will be lighter, more joyful and more grateful in our daily lives. We will also be able to offer our love in the most sincere way without expecting anything in return, as well as surrendering more to True Source.

Surrendering to True Source is very important in our relationship with True Source. Surrendering to True Source is needed when we are offering our love with sincerity without expecting anything in return, as well as in other areas of our life. We need to surrender to True Source in all aspects without exception: for example, to surrender all of our desires and interests when going through different life experiences, until we can surrender our whole self completely to True Source. Only after we surrender our whole self to True Source can we be brought to return to True Source completely by True Source Love.

It may be slightly confusing for some of you and you may wonder if we are allowed to have any desires? How about our basic needs, such as shelter, food and our family's needs? We will discuss this topic more deeply in a separate chapter **(Chapter 15)**.

F. The Sixth Key: Using Every Moment in Life to Choose True Source

Please remember that life is not a coincidence. Life is a gift of Love, personally given by True Source to help our spirit choose True Source. Even the roles that we face, everything we go through, our condition, etc was chosen by True Source to give the best for each of us. It is time we start to realize this and be grateful to True Source. We can then start to use our life according to True Source beautiful Plan - which is to choose True Source - so our true self (our spirit) can be brought to return to True Source and to be joyful with True Source eternally.

G. The Seventh Key: Being Grateful Every Moment to True Source

Being grateful to True Source sounds simple and very familiar as this topic is a common subject for many people. However, being grateful to True Source wholeheartedly, and especially every moment, is a very important matter in our relationship with True Source.

H. The Eight Key: Sharing True Source Love with All Beings

By now, if we are still focused on ourselves, it is time we realize that True Source Love is for all beings. Simply thinking about these things is definitely not enough. Everything must be expressed with the proper heart attitude by being True Source instruments in our daily lives.

As the discussion of spirituality is profound, the explanation or categorization (keys) may be different depending on the topic that is being discussed. What I write and discuss in this book may not be exactly the same as in other books I have previously written such as:

Smile to your Heart Meditation: Simple practices for peace, Health, and Spiritual Growth and **The real you: Beyond Forms and Lives**, and so on. Do not merely compare the words or remember my explanation word for word. It is through these different perspectives and differing explanations and words, that I hope that you will be able to understand everything more clearly and, most importantly, will be able to capture the essence.

Chapter 11
The First Key:
Using Our Heart

The importance of the heart in our relationship with True Source has been mentioned in many holy and ancient books. At the beginning, our spirit was close to True Source, but then we chose to leave True Source and rejected the direct help from True Source in returning completely to True Source. If we now say that we want to choose True Source, do not make a hasty conclusion, because it is our mind saying so. Even if we do everything that we are supposed to do, our duties, acts of worship and charity to the best of our ability, without using the heart, all of our efforts will not improve the relationship of our spirit with True Source. This is because our brain and physical bodies are only temporary. One day, our physical body and brain will die and become ash and dust. Our spirit, however, will exist eternally. Even though I have discussed the information about the heart in my other book titled, **Smile to Your Heart Meditations: Simple practices for Peace, Health and Spiritual Growth**, as this discussion is very important, then there is no harm in discussing it more deeply.

A. Our Heart

The Heart we referring to here is something non-physical within the chest cavity – refer to *Illustration 30*. So, we are not referring to the physical heart.

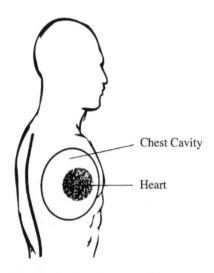

Chest Cavity

Heart

Illustration 30: The Spiritual Heart Within the Chest Cavity

Without using our heart, none of our good deeds, prayers, etc. can reach our true self.

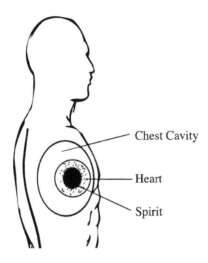

Illustration 31: *The True Self/Spirit within the Spiritual Heart*

Our heart is our key connection with True Source, because it is within our heart that our spirit/true self resides *(Refer to Illustration 31)*. Our spirit/true self is also often referred to as the spark of True Source. Even though our spirit left True Source, True Source still showed love and care for us by giving us "another us", which is our physical body and our brain. Only by using our heart can the actions of our physical body and brain connect and reach our spirit and therefore impact our relationship with True Source.

Even though our spirit is reluctant in the beginning, when we pray to True Source with our heart, the spirit that resides within our heart cannot reject, run, or turn away from True Source. Our spirit will also be directed even more to True Source and accept True Source Love. That is the reason True Source created our heart as the special facility to connect not only our spirit with True Source but also our other parts, which are our physical body and non-physical body layers.

Therefore, without using the heart, whatever we do will not reach our spirit, because our heart also acts as a fortress that prevents us from doing anything to our spirit. Whatever we do to our spirit will be catastrophic. That is why True Source gave us the gift of our truly special heart, which we cannot harm or damage. As soon as we surrender to True Source, then True Source Love can instantly do all the most beautiful things to our heart–and at the same time do all the most beautiful things to our spirit.

Other than that, we also know that our spirit does not need earthly knowledge because everything earthly is just temporary. For our spirit there is only one vitally important matter, which is our relationship with The Creator. It is clear that the important key in what we do is to **use our heart** to be closer to True Source.

To be even clearer, let us view this situation from a different perspective. Once you recognize that our spirit resides within our heart and that as a human we can only be connected with our spirit through our heart, what do you presume is happening when we pray to True Source without using our heart? When we are praying, it is clear that this physical body is praying to True Source. But, because we do not use the heart, our spirit will not join in the prayer. Our spirit is eternal, while our physical body can be referred to as only the "outer layer", "skin", or "clothes". When our physical body and mind are praying to True Source, it does not mean that the non-physical body layers and soul are also praying. Our soul is a different consciousness and, although it is attached to our physical body and brain, our soul may not be in harmony with our brain. Only when we are using our heart properly can our non-physical body layers, soul and spirit also pray to True Source all together. This is why we need to use our heart as often as possible in our relationship with True Source. This takes on a special importance if we would like to use our whole lives in accordance with the true purpose of our lives, which is for our spirit to be closer to True Source, in order to return completely to True Source.

As a note, after you understand these matters, then you will be able to realize simply and clearly how all stories or exercises related to the spirit or true self, which fail to mention the heart, are not proper. The spirit resides within the heart and cannot be touched by us at all. How can someone communicate or do things to their spirit without going through the heart? Non-physical matters are not visible to the naked eye; hence it may be confusing for some people. Some may feel they have an idea or may conduct experiments without knowing the proper direction. Even though those experiments may produce interesting sensations or experiences, this does not mean that they are proper. On the contrary, when we do use our heart and Inner Heart just to surrender to True Source, then it is not possible for anything to be incorrect and, it produces something that is very beautiful on earth as well as in the afterlife.

B. Why Our Heart is so Special

Our heart is True Source's special creation. It serves as a connecting facility between True Source, our spirit and other parts that help our spirit to be closer to True Source. So, it is not an exaggeration to say that our heart is special. This is especially true as no other beings, methods or powers can help us to be closer to True Source. Only we can dirty or do negative things to our heart and only True Source can cleanse or do the best things for our heart. Another special quality of the heart is that whatever good is happening on our heart will also instantly happen on our spirit that resides in our heart, as well as the main spirit in the void.

Isn't it so beautiful to know that the special qualities of the heart, gifted by True Source, really helps us to achieve the true purpose of our lives? We cannot go wrong because only True Source knows the best and the most beautiful for our lives. This will facilitate our journey because we do not need to struggle to do anything to our spirit. We only need to focus on our heart and use it as a facility to connect and communicate with The Creator in order to be closer to, choose and prioritize True Source.

Even though we know that our heart is the key to helping our spirit with the true purpose of our lives and that we must surrender our heart to True Source, it does not mean that we can use our heart to surrender to True Source straight away. Our Heart must be opened and cleansed first. The best and easiest way is for us to do the steps in **Heart Strengthening** and **Open Heart Prayer**. I have discussed these two matters in great detail in my other books. However, it will be my pleasure to discuss it again in this book.

1. Strengthening our Heart

This practice is simply a natural method to strengthen your heart. Although it seems straightforward this is a very important and beneficial practice to help in strengthening your heart, mainly so that:

- The attention towards the Heart increases
- The domination of the brain lessens
- The Heart and the feeling become stronger

We will invite you to close your eyes so that your brain is relaxed. You will therefore need to read and remember the steps that you will need to do. Of course the process of memorizing the practice steps will require effort from the mind and make it less relaxed. To overcome this situation, you can record the instructions of the steps and then just play your recording when you are practicing. This way, when you practice, you will be really relaxed without needing to remember the steps that you need to do. *You will only need to listen to the instructions from the recording.*

Before practicing, find a quiet place. You can sit on a chair or sit cross-legged on the floor, depending on which is more comfortable for you. It is best if the seat you choose is not too softly padded so your body is calmer when practicing. Try to ensure that your spine is quite straight, without being tense. The easiest way is to have a seat with back support that is straight and hard with your bottom as close as possible to the back of the chair. The most important thing is to ensure you continue to be relaxed and enjoy this practice without any expectations.

When you are ready:
- Relax so that your brain is not tense
- Close your eyes to further reduce the activity of your brain
- Touch your heart with one or two fingers
- Smile freely to your heart without thinking of how or where
- With your eyes still closed, continue to relax and smile to your heart (about 1 minute). If thoughts start to surface, do not follow them. Continue to relax.
- You will start to feel an expanding feeling/calmness/peace/lightness/joy in your chest.
- As you start to feel one or more of these feelings, they are an

indication that your heart is starting to be activated. Follow your feeling so that your heart and feeling can become stronger

- For those of you who do not yet feel anything, do not try to do anything. All you need to do is continue to relax and smile. When your brain stops trying or searching, you will start to feel one or more of the feelings mentioned above. So, continue being relaxed and smiling freely.

- As soon as you feel something, follow that feeling while continuously being relaxed and smiling freely. Enjoy (2 minutes+)

2. Open Heart Prayer

Other than repeating the heart strengthening practice several times, it would be very beneficial to you if you also do this Open Heart prayer. Remember that a huge number of negativities arise from negative emotions that have accumulated in our hearts over many years. We need to cleanse this accumulation of negativities so there will be room to accept True Source Love.

Only True Source's Blessing can open our heart and, because of that, we will rely solely on True Source Love in prayers. Do this prayer while sitting down on a chair or on the floor with comfortable padding. Your spine needs to be quite straight without forcing yourself. If you are sitting on the floor, it is best that you sit cross-legged. If you are sitting on a chair, you can lean on the chair as long as your spine is straight.

The essence of this opening heart process is to pray to True Source. In order for our prayer to True Source to be from our hearts, we will do a few preparation steps before we start praying. Overall, this process is called **Open Heart Meditation**[4].

a. Sitting down relaxed...your spine quite straight...without forcing yourself

b. Place your palms on your lap, facing upwards

c. Close your eyes so your mind is not too active

d. Relax...and smile...let your whole mind and self be here...and now...to do this open heart meditation properly.

e. While still being relaxed and smiling, take a deep breath without forcing yourself...exhale from your mouth...let all burdens and thoughts be released together with your breath...and feel your whole body becoming more relaxed...Feel...and enjoy these moments as your whole self is becoming more relaxed...and smile freely

f. Inhale deeply...exhale from your mouth...let all burdens and thoughts be released together with your breath...and feel your whole body becoming more relaxed...Feel...and enjoy these moments your whole self is becoming more relaxed...and smile more freely

---

[4] Even though it includes the word "meditation" in this exercise, from several perspectives, this exercise is very different to meditation in general.
Some of the differences include:

• In this exercise, we are not "empty". We want to be relaxed, but not "empty".
• We will rely on The Love of True Source completely

Detailed explanations and a variety of exercises to strengthen, open and use the Heart can be found in the book Smile to Your Heart Meditations: Simple Practices for Peace, Health & Spiritual Growth.

Open Heart Meditation can be downloaded on itunes and cdbaby.com or you can contact any of our representatives.

g. Inhale deeply...and exhale from your mouth...let all the leftover burdens and thoughts as well as any tension in your body be released together with your breath...and now feel your whole body and mind becoming very relaxed...enjoy...and smile while enjoying these moments when your body and mind are relaxed...from now on breathe normally...that is by inhaling and exhaling from your nose

h. Now, place either one or both your palms in the middle of your chest...where your heart is located...and smile to your heart...do not think or try to search where exactly your heart is...All you need to do is to smile freely...while listening to these instructions

i. Continue to smile freely to your heart...with all your feeling...feel you are becoming calmer...enjoy...while still smiling...Moments like these you are letting your heart become stronger

j. While still placing both your palms on your chest and smiling to your heart and enjoying the calmness from your heart...let us now pray to ask for True Source Love so the emotions within our heart can be cleansed and our heart can be opened wider to True Source. When praying, you do not need to repeat the sentences. Let your heart do the prayer because that is the best

True Source, please bless our heart so that all arrogance is replaced with Your Love

True Source, please bless our heart so that all anger is replaced with Your Love

True Source, please bless our heart so that all selfishness is replaced with Your Love

True Source, please bless our heart so that all envy and jealousy are replaced with Your Love

True Source, please bless our heart so that all cunningness and greediness are replaced with Your Love

True Source, please bless and help us to realize that our heart is our key connection to You... we must keep our heart clean because our connection with you is the most important... please bless and help us to be able to forgive others...sincerely...

(Now, forgive everyone who has done you wrong, even if the same person/same people are still doing so, remember that our connection to True Source is the most important) {1 minute}

True Source, now that we have forgiven everyone who has done us wrong, please bless our heart so that all hatred, grudges, resentment, hurt feelings, dissatisfaction, and all other negative emotions are removed from our heart to be replaced with Your Love

True Source, please bless and help us to be able to realize all of our wrongdoings to You and to others...please help us to be remorseful and ask for Your Forgiveness sincerely...

*(Now, realize all of our wrongdoings to True Source and to others,
be remorseful and ask for forgiveness from True Source)*
{1 minute}
*True Source, please forgive us for all of our wrongdoings to You and to
others, and now that you have forgiven us, please bless and help so
that all burdens, fear, worries, and other related negative emotions
because of our mistakes and wrongdoings be removed from our whole
heart and our whole self to be replaced with Your Love*
*True Source, please bless our heart, so that all worries and fears
caused by our lack of trust in You are removed, to be replaced with Your
Love*
*True Source, as our heart has been cleansed from so many negative
emotions...please bless our heart to open even better to You... to be
directed better to You... Let Your Love flow more abundantly into our
heart so that the feelings from our heart become stronger, so that we can
feel the calmness.... peace...and the beauty of Your Love even better...*
*True Source, please let Your Love fill our whole heart and whole self...
so that our whole heart and whole self are filled with calmness... and
peace... so that we can let Your Love help us even more... to always use
our heart... within Your Love...*
*True Source... Thank You for Your Love... that has cleansed all
negative emotions from our heart and self... that has opened and
directed our heart even better to You... so that our whole heart and
self are filled with Your Love even more... so that we can feel and
enjoy the calmness... peacefulness... and the beauty of Your Love even
better*
Thank You, True Source....Amen...

k. let one or both palms stay on your chest...while still smiling... feel your heart and self becoming lighter and lighter...enjoy...let yourself continue to be within this calmness and peacefulness... these are moments you are within your heart...continue to smile while enjoying.

l. While still smiling...enjoying...let yourself be immersed and dissolve within the calmness and peacefulness from True Source Love...so that your heart becomes stronger...and you dissolve more and more within True Source Love...Feel...the more you immerse and dissolve within the calmness and peacefulness... your heart feels lighter and more beautiful...enjoy

m. While still smiling and enjoying the calmness, peacefulness, and the beauty of True Source Love, slowly...move your fingers and open your eyes with a smile...let yourself go through your daily life while still being within your heart...within the calmness and peacefulness from True Source Love.

Notes:

- The prayer within the meditation given here is just as an example. You are free to use terminologies and words you are most comfortable with.
- Open Heart Meditation is not intended to replace the prayers you usually do.
- For the best result, do this meditation twice a day. Firstly, do this meditation in the morning so your heart is calmer, more peaceful and lighter in your daily life. Then, do it once again in the evening or at night after you have completed your activities so

that all the excessive thoughts or burdens can be cleansed. You will feel calmer and more peaceful and will be able to sleep more deeply and wake up fresher the next day. However, if you do not have enough time to do this meditation twice a day, just doing it once a day regularly will also give you benefits after you do it consecutively for several days. You will be able to feel that your heart and your whole self is calmer, more peaceful and lighter.

After doing these two exercises properly for just a few times, you will be able to feel the benefits. Usually, you will feel lighter, calmer, more peaceful and even more joyful. For those of you who are more sensitive, you will be able to feel a light sensation or an open space in your chest area. This is because your heart has opened more, become cleaner and is filled with True Source Love. When you pray you will be able to feel a noticeable difference. You will be able to feel the very beautiful direct connection with True Source.

The heart is without a doubt the key to our connection with True Source. As soon as our heart is opened, then our direct connection to True Source will be reconnected. Previously, our heart was filled with negativities from our negative emotions in our daily life. Every time we have negative emotions, whether it is anger, arrogance, jealousy, envy, grudges, sadness or whatever it may be, our heart will instantly be contaminated. Unfortunately, in our daily lives, we experience this numerous times. After you have strengthened your heart and you continue with open heart prayer, then True Source Love can start to cleanse your heart and you will feel the results clearly.

Opening and using the heart is also beneficial, not only for our spirit, but also within our daily life. We will experience positive feelings such as feeling calmer, more peaceful, feeling closer to True Source and so on. Other than that, we can be more focused at work, have brilliant ideas, and still carry out our daily responsibilities. Our interaction with others will also improve greatly. Being close to True Source, being loved, protected, guided: isn't that the most beautiful thing we can receive?

As a note, when someone opens their heart, whether they are still alive or have passed away, it does not guarantee that they have no remaining attachments or burdens at all. An open heart connects someone directly to The Creator through The Love that is continuously given to all beings. With an open heart, True Source Love can easily help to cleanse and let go of attachments and burdens instantly, no matter how intense they may be. Hence, an open heart is a facility.

The next question is whether the person is using this facility or not? As an example, if you choose to walk even though you have a car, you are not using your car. In relation to the heart that has already been opened, even though our heart is filled more with calmness, peacefulness and other beautiful things, we are not perfect beings. Often, for one reason or another, we will react with our negative emotions. Whether we choose to surrender our negative emotions completely to choose True Source or we follow those emotions, is our own choice entirely. What we need to do in this life, other than opening and using our heart, is to always choose True Source completely.

The Open Heart Prayer that I have shared helps us to cleanse those negative emotions from our heart. Even though doing the Open Heart Prayer wholeheartedly is beneficial, it is not enough. Choosing True Source more completely every moment is the true purpose of our lives.

C. Using our Heart

Our heart is very important as the first key to open the "real way" that has been provided by True Source. Without opening and using our heart, everything we do is the product of our brain, which is not the best and, more importantly, does not improve the connection between our true self and True Source. Remember that our life is a facility, given personally by True Source, to help our true selves.

We must always use our heart. The way to use our heart is by doing the Open Heart prayer every day so that our heart becomes cleaner and more opened to True Source. Do the exercise to strengthen the heart before praying often, because by doing the steps to strengthen the heart, our heart that has been limited for a long time can automatically, start to be used.

You will feel a significant change if you do it properly. You will also be able to clearly feel the direct loving connection from True Source to you when you pray to True Source. You will be able to feel how your heart and whole self are moved so deeply when you call True Source. Your feeling and mind will be filled with calmness, peacefulness and joy. Your negative emotions will gradually diminish and automatically you will see and face various situations in a completely new way.

However, our relationship with True Source is extremely deep, especially if we are talking about the true purpose of life. In order to attain the true purpose of life, we will next discuss other important keys to be able to use "the real way" that has been personally provided by True Source for all.

D. The Condition of the Spirit

The condition of our spirit is more or less the same as the condition of our heart. Whatever happens to our heart happens instantly to our spirit and vice versa. Thus, to know the condition of our spirit, all we have to do is to look at the condition of our heart. I would like to remind you that many people who I have met feel that they have already opened and used their hearts in their daily life, especially those who are quite wholehearted in praying, doing good deeds, charity and so on.

Of course, if you are diligent in praying and doing good things, we can say that your heart is quite opened and you often use your heart. However, it does not necessarily mean that you have opened and used your heart in the best way possible, bearing in mind that we must open our heart to True Source completely.

There are several fundamental differences between those who have or have not opened and used their heart properly. For those who have opened and used their heart properly:

- In praying, not only do you feel close to True Source but, every time you call True Source, you can really feel the very beautiful and clear direct loving connection with True Source. The heart is also moved deeply by longing and the joy of True Source Love
- The heart is filled with light feelings, joy, calmness and peacefulness. If you feel strong impulses or elements, even though the label may be prioritizing True Source, these usually come from the brain.
- You are able to forgive others sincerely and not judge others' weaknesses and shortcomings.

Let us now return to the relationship between our heart and spirit, where the condition of our heart reflects the condition of our spirit as well. How deeply does our heart prioritize True Source and True Source Love in our daily life? Are we living and experiencing life just as a part of our offering of Love to True Source? The condition and attitude of your heart when you were born is the summary of the entire journey you have gone through in your past lives. As we have discussed, what matters is not what we do but rather, how our heart attitude is when we do those things, that is, how our heart prioritizes True Source and whether we are doing so as our offering of Love for True Source.

So, it is not important whether we were royalty, rich, poor, a merchant or whatever else in our most recent past life, as everything is just a facility, a temporary role that has passed. How our heart attitude was when we played that role, in everything that we went through and how we chose True Source, is what will continue on, and is reflected by the condition and attitude of our heart upon birth in this life.

That is why True Source does not give us memories of our past lives. Although some people do remember their past lives, this is not a must. If you are already prepared to go deeper to be acquainted with yourself better, then you may wish to experience some of your past lives. This can help you not only to discover your past profession or to see how famous you were, but also to realize more about your attitudes and habits that have been with you for a long time and still currently exist. We often do not consider our less desirable attitudes or habits as bothersome, because they have been around for a long time. Nevertheless, after re-experiencing some of our past lives, these weaknesses will be even clearer so that we can be more wholehearted in improving them. More information related to this topic can be read in my

Soul Consciousness book.

At this moment, the condition of your heart and spirit will certainly have changed compared to when you were born. Every lifetime is supposed to be an opportunity to improve the condition of our heart and spirit. However, as we have previously discussed, only True Source Love can cleanse and do positive things on our heart and spirit. If you do not open your heart enough and let True Source Love help you, then there is a tendency for the opposite to happen. Remember that every time we have negative emotions or when we are too consumed with our desires, we are contaminating our heart, which will for sure have a negative effect on our heart and spirit.

How about those who have not yet opened their heart or rely on True Source Love enough, but are still diligently doing various positive things such as praying, doing charity work, doing cleansing exercises? As previously mentioned, doing such things is certainly beneficial, but usually only on the physical and non-physical (soul) level. However, the heart and spirit stay the same. Only True Source Love can cleanse and do the most beautiful things. And our heart must be opened to True Source before our heart can receive True Source Love. Furthermore, an open heart is not enough. Our heart should be opened and surrendering to True Source every moment, to be able to accept True Source Love.

Chapter 12
The Second Key:
Using Our Inner Heart

By using our heart, we will be connected to True Source and True Source will be able to help our spirit. We will not only feel an extraordinary change in our relationship with True Source but also in our daily life. We will become closer to True Source in such a beautiful way; but just opening and using our heart in our relationship with True Source and in our daily lives is not enough, especially if we intend to return to True Source completely.

The next step is for us to use our **Inner Heart**. Our Inner Heart is the core of our heart that must be used completely, as a director, so that at the very least:

- The Heart can open more completely to True Source
- We can realize True Source Will (the proper direction)

- We can remember and long for True Source from our own hearts and Inner Hearts
- We can trust and surrender more easily to True Source

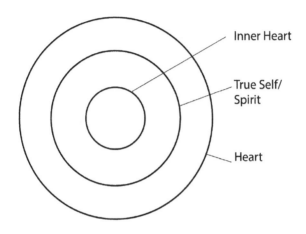

Illustration 32: The Inner Heart and the True Self/Spirit within the Spiritual Heart

In general, we often refer to the spirit as the *"spark"* of True Source. Even I have referred to the spirit as such on numerous occasions in this book. However, as we are discussing this topic more deeply, the core of the spirit that is the inner heart is the true *"spark"* of True Source. *(Refer to Illustration 32)*. So, the inner heart, as the true spark of True Source, has a very special relationship along with a continuous and never ending longing towards True Source. If we consider the special connection between the inner heart and True Source, we may say that the relationship between the heart and True Source is an extension of or an addition to that very special and beautiful relationship which our inner heart, the spark of the Creator, has with the Creator, the source of our Inner Heart.

In other words, from a spiritual perspective, using our inner heart is akin to helping our spirit to use the heart of the spirit. In the past our spirit committed a wrongdoing that made our spirit leave True Source and even up to this very moment, our spirit is still unable to prioritize True Source completely. By using the inner heart properly, that is, by letting the inner heart become the "director" of our whole spirit, heart, and self, then the attitude of our spirit to True Source can change. Only then can our heart open more completely to True Source and will be able to trust and surrender more easily to True Source. For further information, you can refer to my books, **Inner Heart** and **The Real You: Beyond Forms and Lives**.

Even for us as humans, using the inner heart will be very beneficial. Although our direct connection to True Source has been established and continues to improve as we use and open our heart, the inner heart, the very "spark" of True Source within us, is an even more important and deeper key when we discuss our relationship with True Source. By using the heart, with the inner heart as "director", our relationship with True Source will become even more complete and beautiful.

Although the direct connection between our heart and True Source has been established through strengthening our heart and doing Open Heart Meditation every day, the connection between our inner Heart and True Source is deeper and more important, making the proper use of our inner Heart, the real spark of True Source a more important key. By using our Inner Heart as the "director", our connection with True Source becomes more complete and beautiful.

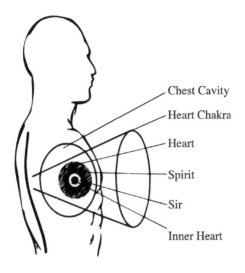

Illustration 33: The Inner Heart, the Sir, the True Self/Spirit and the Spiritual Heart within the Heart Chakra in the Chest Cavity

Using our inner heart is akin to helping our spirit to use the heart of the spirit

Although compared to our mind, our heart knows a lot about the truth, our heart still has limitations. Only our inner heart is unlimited. Through our inner heart, we can realize the truth without any limits. In *Illustration 33*, we can see that our inner heart is encased within the **sir**, which means "secret". This is because if we are connected to our Inner Heart that is encased within the **sir**, we will then be granted access to all secrets.

The way we use the inner heart as director will usually change significantly after someone has attained their true self consciousness. At that very moment, our true consciousness clearly recognizes that the inner heart is the "spark" of True Source, which will be reflected in the spirit's attitude towards True Source. Previously, our spirit knew that our inner heart was the "spark", but this knowledge was not yet reflected in the spirit's attitude. That is why our spirit left True Source and although True Source wanted to help our spirit directly, our spirit refused to be helped.

Reaching our true self consciousness is a very important stage, spiritually speaking. However, several other books express the belief that reaching this stage is the same as reaching one's true purpose of life. Unfortunately this belief is incorrect. Although this attainment is a major step, it is not in itself sufficient to be able to trust and surrender completely to True Source and return to True Source completely. Nevertheless, spiritually speaking, after reaching true self consciousness, if all of the realizations are used properly, we will usually be able to accept and let True Source Love bring our soul even to beyond the highest heaven after passing away. Even though we will not yet have attained the real purpose of life, reaching the highest heaven will give us the opportunity to continuously put into practice what we have learned and realized, without having to reincarnate again.

What do I mean by this? Aren't life and incarnations gifts of Love from True Source to help our spirit return completely to True Source? Why am I now saying that one may not need to be reborn but still have the chance to continue one's journey to return to True Source completely?

Please remember that True Source is the All Loving. True Source has continuously wanted to help us since before our first incarnation, long before the earth, galaxies, the universe, heaven or even hell were created by True Source. It was our spirit who rejected True Source Love and Help. So, if our attitude reaches a level where we accept all the help given by True Source, including all the gifts of Love to change our attitude in trusting and surrendering to True Source. Then even after death, our "spiritual journey", which is our journey to return to True Source completely, can continue without having to be reborn. Naturally, it would be best if we would continuously let our whole self be helped completely by True Source while we are still alive to be able to return to True Source completely.

Chapter 13
The Third Key: Trusting True Source Completely

After we open and use our heart with Inner Heart as the director, our relationship with True Source will change significantly. Our realization about True Source Love will also change because we will have experienced everything first hand with our own heart. If everything related to True Source and True Source Love had previously always been a mere concept for our very limited brain, then it will now have changed. Our Heart and Inner Heart are the very facilities given by True Source personally for our relationship with True Source. Our Heart and Inner Heart can directly feel and experience True Source Love clearly, as well as realize many things related to True Source Love that were previously only concepts or theories.

Trusting True Source more completely will become easier and more natural. For example, understandings about:

- The One and Only True Source
- True Source the Almighty

- True Source the All Loving
- True Source Will for us to return to True Source
- True Source Love that can remove our negative karma
- True Source does not expect us to be perfect, but for us just to be willing to be helped, loved and cared for by True Source

A. The One and Only True Source

If we put our complete trust in True Source, it will only be natural to acknowledge that there is only One True Source, The One and Only Creator of all beings. There is no other Creator.

B. True Source the Almighty

We will realize more and more how True Source is the Almighty. If we do not trust that True Source is the Almighty, we will not believe that True Source can help us and that True Source Love can really do the most beautiful things for us, now and eternally.

C. True Source the All Loving

Although we have read over and over again that True Source is the All Loving, this realization will need some time and firsthand experience to settle. Usually, this understanding will be clearer once we have opened our heart to True Source and can directly feel True Source Love for us by ourselves. Feeling and experiencing True Source Love first hand within, or through, our heart is extremely different to simply reading or talking about True Source Love. Even if we write thousands of books about True Source Love, it will never compare to our direct personal experience in feeling True Source Love for us through our heart.

D. True Source Will for us to Return to True Source

Although many of us do believe in True Source, we sometimes hold on to the concept that it is True Source Will for us to struggle, in order to live our lives in the best possible way. If you have personally felt True Source Love with your heart, then your realization about this matter will blossom on its own. You will realize more and more how True Source has given abundant Love to help us in living our lives in the most beautiful way. Look at the abundance of beautiful gifts of love that you have been given to complete your journey: the people you love around you, beautiful trees, various flowers in all shapes and colors. Everything exists only because True Source really gives us the best in our journey to return to True Source completely.

It is certainly true that we need to be committed to use our life, which is a beautiful gift of Love from True Source, properly. If we are not wholehearted, then we will just go back and forth and fail to use our life in the best way possible.

E. True Source Love can Remove our Negative Karma

Trusting True Source also means that we must trust and realize how True Source Love is extraordinary. Our karma is the result of our actions in the existence. True Source Love is far above anything in the existence. True Source Love can reduce or even erase our negative karma completely and thoroughly. Without trusting and realizing this

139

matter, our heart and whole being will not be able to return to True Source completely. Otherwise, whether we realize it or not, parts of us will be occupied in trying to take care of things we assume are important, such as cleansing our negative karma.

Let us now look at the situation from a bigger perspective. The real us is the spirit, the "spark" of True Source. Our spirit cannot get sick. Our spirit cannot die. Yet, to help our spirit that refused to be helped directly by True Source, we were given this temporary physical body that will for sure experience various problems or illnesses and will ultimately die.

This is a part of True Source Will so that we, with our limitations, with our problems and weaknesses, will start to look for True Source. True Source has also given us a heart that has been personally created and bestowed to us, with a part within our heart that always longs to find True Source Love. Without finding True Source Love, our heart will always feel empty, like something is missing.

Hence, we look for True Source. Praying to True Source to ask for help with our problems, needs, weaknesses and hopes is not wrong. On the contrary, it is very good and how it ought to be, as long as we use our heart. When we use our heart to pray to True Source and after our heart has been touched directly by True Source, our relationship with True Source will change. If previously we only looked for True Source when we needed something (for our own interests), this attitude will change after being touched by True Source Love. We will now remember True Source and pray to True Source, even though we do not need anything. We will remember and pray to True Source to express our gratitude and in our longing for True Source.

F. True Source does not Expect us to be Perfect, but for us just to be Willing to be Helped, Loved and Cared for by True Source

Although we are aware that we have many weaknesses, the way we act shows how we forget that we are beings with many weaknesses. Unwittingly, we often act as if we are trying to be a perfect being. It is true that some people believe becoming perfect is the purpose of life or the true spiritual journey.

I hope that you do not become one of the many people who believe so. We are imperfect beings. Who are we, as imperfect beings to know the path or way to reach perfection? We do not even know true perfection, how can we know the path to perfection? Only True Source, the Source of All Perfection, can grant us that perfection as a Gift of Love from True Source.

So, with all of our weaknesses, how are we to choose True Source and become closer to True Source? Remember only True Source can help us become closer to True Source. Even if we become more perfect, it does not mean that we are becoming closer to True Source. All we need to do is always remember True Source and have trust in True Source unlimited Love. We can use every one of our weaknesses as a facility to rely on True Source Love and be willing to be helped by True Source Love always.

If this is done properly, the upcoming chapter about surrendering will help us to remember better and to open our heart to accept True Source Love. This will automatically bring us closer to True Source. If we take every opportunity to use our weaknesses as facilities, our whole heart and self will always remember True Source and prioritize True Source.

141

At those very moments, we will be loved continuously by True Source and be as close as possible to True Source.

On the other hand, if we seek perfection, even by relying on True Source Love, we will still not be able to eliminate our distance with True Source. We do not need to be perfect. It is better to use our weaknesses just as a facility to prioritize True Source.

Help from Other Beings

Although I have clearly emphasized that every being, including all humans, should only ever pray to and praise True Source, I have added this section to complement your understanding so you can better understand the reasons behind it. True Source, the All Loving, is always forgiving. However, the consequences of praying or getting help from other non-physical beings are detrimental to our spirit. Irrespective of whether or not we have opened or used our heart, if we pray to or ask for help from other non-physical beings, our spirit will turn towards those beings, in other words, our spirit will turn away from True Source.

Unfortunately, as we know, it is not easy to do positive things spiritually. On the contrary, often it seems easier to do negative things. For example, our spirit refuses to be helped by True Source. Without using the heart, our spirit will not accept True Source help or, in other words, no positive effect is happening on our spirit. However, if someone prays or asks for help from a non-physical being, the spirit will certainly be affected, without having to use the heart.

It is More Difficult to get Help from True Source

We also need to know that there are people who pray to or seek help from other beings and say it is much easier for them to get what they want that way as opposed to praying to True Source. It is time we believe that True Source is the Almighty, All Loving and All Caring who for sure always gives us the best. Remember again how True Source chose this exact role and life that we have. Often, there are different situations that we have to experience according to the lessons that we need. Usually, those that are not the best are related to our own mistakes that we have made in our past lives.

Because of the mistakes that we have made in our past lives, it is possible that something that we need or hope for in this lifetime is not yet achieved. In general, people will say that we need to do a lot of good deeds to create positive karma and reduce or redeem the negative karma that we have created in our past lives. Even though this method may work, the best way is just to realize how True Source loves each and every one of us and wants to help us with all of our weaknesses. With this realization, if we can surrender our wants, needs and hopes to wholeheartedly prioritize True Source and True Source Love, then we can accept the most beautiful gifts of Love from True Source. This will not only reduce or erase the negative karma from what we did in our past lives, but will also help us with our needs and hopes.

On the other hand, if we seek help from other beings, we may initially seem to get what we need or hope for. Unfortunately, the underlying causes of why those needs and hopes were not met (because we did not pray to True Source) have not been addressed. When this happens, even though we feel satisfied because the help of other beings fulfilled what we needed, we have not advanced spiritually at all. Realizing that the true purpose of our lives is to return completely to True Source, we also recognize that achieving our wants and hopes through the help of other beings does not bring us closer to True Source at all. Instead, turning to another being is taking us further away from True Source because our spirit is turning away from True Source to face that being.

Remember that we are beings that are full of limitations and, whether we realize it or not, we also have many wants, which are usually not good for us. If what we want is something that is not good for us, True Source will for sure not give it to us no matter how much we pray to True Source, because True Source is the All Knowing, who knows what is best for everyone. It is clear that other beings do not know what is best for our lives.

It is time we realize that there is only one True Source, The Creator, The Source of our true selves and our only destiny. Even angels, exalted and holy beings are only the subjects of True Source who are also on the journey to return completely to True Source. Maybe some of you have tried to pray to True Source but you are not sure whether your prayer has been accepted by True Source. Open your heart to True Source and pray to True Source using your heart, then you will be able to clearly feel how your prayer is accepted. True Source, the All Loving and All Caring, is always listening, guiding, helping, loving and caring for us.

If you can have a direct relationship with True Source, the Source and Destiny of all beings, why waste it on your personal interests? As our lives are just facilities to help us to return completely to True Source, do not turn away from True Source to satisfy wants that usually relate to something temporary. Our relationship with True Source is eternal. Always remember that True Source is the Source of Love, The Source of Health, The Source of Happiness, The Source of Wealth and The

Source of everything good. Do not seek help or rely on anyone else other than True Source. It is better not to get something that we hope for, whatever it may be, as long as it does not bring us further away from True Source. Our true purpose of life is to improve our relationship with True Source.

All we need to do is always remember True Source and have trust in True Source unlimited Love. We can use every one of our weaknesses as a facility to rely on True Source Love and be willing to be helped by True Source Love always.

Chapter 14
Fourth Key: The Direction is to Be Loved and Taken Care of by True Source

Even though we say that we trust True Source to help with all of our weaknesses and we pray to True Source, we are often merely paying lip service. We still have the tendency to limit True Source Love and to prioritize ourselves. If we use the three keys that we have discussed properly, that is, using our Heart, Inner Heart and trusting True Source, our relationship with True Source can change. Isn't it clear now that we can really understand and realize through our heart and inner heart what it means to say that True Source is All Loving, that True Source truly always gives us the best and that True Source does not expect us to be perfect, but just to be willing to be helped, loved and cared for by True Source.

The important key in our relationship with True Source is to be loved and taken care of by True Source. In everything we do, we always need to let True Source Love help us so the direction is only to be loved and taken care of by True Source. If we don't, even if we are doing something that is in accordance to True Source Will, there will be a tendency for us to do those things in our own way, not really for True Source. Even in relying on True Source Love, we may still be doing so for our own interests; in other words, we are just utilizing True Source Love for our own interests.

This may sound confusing. Isn't relying on True Source Love a positive thing? This is especially true if we are referring to relying on True Source Love to be closer to and returning to True Source, which is the Will of True Source. If that is True Source Will, what's the difference or what's wrong with doing it for our own interest? Although speaking from an earthly perspective it looks the same, spiritually speaking, the two are very different.

If we are doing something for our own interests, then we are the priority, not True Source. Our heart is directed to ourselves, not to True Source. Although we may think that we are doing so to trust, to be closer or to return to True Source completely, all of those good intentions are unfortunately just lip service. Within, everything we do is still related to our own interests and ourselves. However, to be closer to, and especially to return to True Source, it needs to be the other way around. That means that our heart should be ever more completely directed to True Source and prioritizing True Source wholeheartedly. That is why we need to surrender all of our interests to True Source and not be fooled by these seemingly 'sweet' titles that masquerade as True Source Will.

Sometimes our brain thinks that we really are being wholehearted in wanting to prioritize True Source and we are committed in wanting to surrender our desires. Unfortunately the deeper parts within us are still rejecting True Source. The easiest way to change these deeper parts is by praying to True Source so that everything we do is just in the direction of being loved by True Source. If we rely on True Source Love with our Heart and Inner Heart, and routinely pray to True Source so that everything we do, including those things we do to become closer to and return to True Source are done only to be loved by True Source, then gradually our interests can be taken care of by True Source.

Let us begin with a simple example that we have previously discussed, such as doing charitable deeds. We might pray to True Source so we can do our charity work sincerely to:

1. Become closer to True Source
2. Surrender to True Source more and more
3. Be loved by True Source more and more

It is very important and beautiful to pray to True Source so we can be sincere in doing our charity work. This relates back to what we previously discussed regarding our many weaknesses. By relying on True Source Love, True Source Love can help us to do the best without weaknesses. In this example of doing charity work, there is a difference between praying to True Source so we can be sincere in doing our work in order to be closer to True Source, as opposed to surrendering more and more, or praying to be loved more and more by True Source.

All three have very good and deep purposes. However, if you often use your Heart and Inner Heart and are able to feel, you will realize that the first two purposes - to pray to True Source to be sincere in doing our charity to be closer to True Source and to surrender more to True Source- still have limitations. The deepest parts of our heart and spirit are still prioritizing ourselves, and have not yet let go of those matters that we still prioritize. Our heart attitude can begin to change only when we pray to True Source to be sincere in doing our charity to be loved by True Source. The deepest parts of our heart and spirit will then start to let go of our interests and be directed towards True Source more and more completely.

As this is one of the very important keys, please remember it when we are discussing the fifth key, surrendering to True Source. We can only surrender more completely according to True Source Will if we pray with the purpose of being loved by True Source.

Chapter 15
Fifth Key: Surrendering to True Source

Surrendering to True Source is a vital element in our relationship with True Source. Even though I place surrendering to True Source as the fifth key, surrendering to True Source is one of the main elements. Even to open our heart, which I mentioned as the first key, we would need to initially surrender to True Source. That is why I mentioned over and over again that we cannot do anything to our heart and that only True Source Love can give the best. So that is why we should just let True Source Love work completely.

The discussions in this book are quite deep. The term surrendering that is used here does not refer to the concept of surrendering that is generally known by the public. Therefore, we need to understand the way in which true surrendering is related to other realizations. For example, how can we surrender to True Source if we do not trust True Source? How can we surrender to True Source if we are not being loved properly by True Source? Without all of these realizations, surrendering to True Source will only be a theory.

WHEN DO WE NEED TO SURRENDER TO TRUE SOURCE?

Surrendering without the heart will not work. We need to realize that surrendering is not only praying to True Source to let True Source Love work. There are parts of us (our spirit) that are not yet wholeheartedly accepting True Source Love or are even still busy when we are praying to True Source. To improve these conditions, which will automatically improve our relationship with True Source, we need to let True Source Love help us in the following matters:

1. When We Need Something

As I have previously discussed, we need to trust True Source, trust that True Source is Almighty and All Loving. As True Source is Almighty then certainly True Source can give the very best and, as True Source is All Loving, then True Source will always love us and will want to give us everything that is most beautiful even without our needing to ask. After you open and use your heart, you can feel and realize all of this clearly.

With this realization, we need to know that when we need something, it is True Source will for us to remember True Source unlimited Love and to pray to True Source. However, we need to surrender the result, whatever it may be. As we do so, we will feel at peace in our heart and in our lives. Surrendering to True Source in this situation can also be seen as not forcing our desires. On the contrary, we are more accepting as an expression of our trust to True Source.

2. When We Pray or let True Source Love Work

When we are praying or letting True Source Love work and surrendering to True Source, we are not forcing our hopes at all. This is the real proof of an attitude that shows we trust True Source. It shows that we trust that True

Source the Almighty is also the All Loving who wants to give us the most beautiful things. It is not our prayers or what we do that can give us those beautiful things. Every beautiful thing can only be accepted as a Gift of Love.

That is why we should not force our hopes or desires. If we are busy, our heart will also be busy with our prayers, our desires. Our heart will not prioritize True Source or be directed towards True Source, so that even if True Source wants to help or give us those beautiful things, we are the ones who are unable to accept it. We need to pray to True Source wholeheartedly, with our inner heart as director completely. Yet our prayer is only a facility for us to stop our daily busyness and for our heart to be completely directed to True Source and prioritizing True Source, so that we can accept True Source Love. Our prayer is not at all an effort to fulfill our needs.

3. Every Moment

Surrendering to True Source when we need something or when we pray to True Source is just the beginning. Our surrendering to True Source should be in everything and every situation without any exception. However, because surrendering to True Source is quite difficult, it is nearly impossible for us to be able to surrender to True Source in every moment. This will be discussed further in the next chapter.

MATTERS RELATED TO SURRENDERING

To be able to really surrender to True Source more in accordance with True Source Will, we also need to discuss the following matters that from an earthly perspective are closely related to surrendering:

• Following your Inner Heart

- Doing your best
- Laziness, surrendering, and giving up

1. Following your Inner Heart

If we use our inner heart in our daily life, then every time we face a situation or we want something, we will be able to feel what our inner heart is saying. Realizing and listening to what our inner heart is saying is very important and beautiful, because we are not receiving advice from an expert, a holy being or just any other being, but rather it is True Source Will through True Source's spark.

Unfortunately, in our daily life, we tend to be too busy prioritizing our desires and interests. When we desire something, we instantly become consumed with our thoughts about those desires. We may not even give ourselves the chance to realize what our inner heart is saying– which actually only takes a few seconds- because we prioritize our desires and interests too much.

However, if we start to remember True Source more, and how beautiful it is to use our inner heart as our director to realize True Source Will, then listening to our inner heart will feel easier. If our inner heart reacts positively to a particular desire or interest, it means that particular desire or interest is according to True Source Will. On the other hand, if our inner heart does not consent to a particular desire or interest, it means that we need to surrender our desires and plans into True Source hands. It is time for us to choose and prioritize True Source, by entrusting our lives to True Source.

To put it frankly, all of our desires that are not in accordance to True Source Will – through the voice of our inner heart – must be surrendered into True Source hands. If our inner heart really does recommend us not to follow our desires and plans, then do not force that desire or plan. The consequences will certainly not be good for our lives. If we do not surrender our desires that are not in accordance to True Source Will, those desires will block our relationship with True Source.

2. Doing Your Best

Our inner heart will never be wrong let alone misdirect us. If our inner heart is aligned with what we want or plan, it does not mean that we become a passive human being who doesn't do anything. We still need to do everything to the best of our ability and complete our efforts by praying to True Source. The most challenging part is to surrender whatever the result may be to True Source. However, how much effort is best? To answer this, fortunately we have been blessed with our inner heart. We can use our inner heart to measure how much effort we should put into achieving the best in our lives.

As an example, you have just graduated from university and you wish to secure a job. Generally, the inner heart will approve of this desire so that you can pursue this hope. How much effort should you put into getting that job? Several days will not be adequate to do the various tasks needed to get a job. You must be consistent in doing all the tasks necessary to be able to seek employment every day and of course remembering to pray to True Source (every day too), until you gain employment. In addition, although you may spend several hours a day looking for a job, once you finish what you need to do for the day, do not continue to be busy thinking about how to find a job. You have already done what you need to do for the day. You need to be relaxed so your heart is not constantly busy, so your heart can receive the Love from True Source.

3. Laziness, Surrendering and Hopelessness

For some people, surrendering is often confused with laziness and hopelessness. To clarify, I will discuss the differences between them in this book. Take the previous example of looking for a job: you still need to complete what you need to do in finding a job and remember to pray every day. If you only do one or the other: not doing your best but still praying or doing your best without praying, then that is called lazy. Sometimes, some people make excuses by saying that they are 'surrendering', while in fact they are being lazy.

Hopelessness is another matter. If you have been trying to find a job for months and are still unsuccessful in obtaining a position and say that you 'surrender' while stopping your efforts in getting a job, this means you are being hopeless. For sure you need a job. You must continue to do your best until you obtain employment. However, during the times you are still seeking, you still need to trust True Source and use every moment of your life to be closer to True Source.

As a note, even though I mention that you need a job and must continue to do your best until you secure one, this is just a general statement. If you have settled down and your partner has more than enough income for your family and your partner does not demand that you work, then you do not need to work. In this case, even though your inner heart says that working feels quite good and you have tried for months but have not yet secured anything, you can surrender your efforts for the time being and spend your time and energy taking care of other things for yourself and your family.

SURRENDERING TO TRUE SOURCE MORE COMPLETELY

Surrendering to True Source is a very deep and even limitless subject. We will now discuss surrendering more deeply, especially in relation to the matters our spirit needs. By surrendering to True Source, you will let True Source Love help you by improving your spirit's condition in its relationship with True Source. We will therefore discuss two important topics:

1. Surrendering our hopes, interests and desires
2. Only to be loved by True Source

Even though our discussion may seem very simple at first glance, it is in fact of the deepest and most fundamental nature, and can be the most challenging to put into action. You may have various opinions related to the topics I have just mentioned above if you are using your brain to think about it. However, it is best if you trust and feel it directly with your whole heart and inner heart as director and do not just analyze it with your brain.

1. Surrendering our Hopes, Interests and Desires

From our previous discussions, it is clear that True Source the Almighty is also the All Loving who always wants to give us the most beautiful. However, in reality, this beauty rarely touches our lives. The three following matters causes this:

- Our past negative deeds
- Not using our heart
- Our heart not surrendering to True Source (not prioritizing True Source and True Source Love)

Remember that True Source wants to help us in relation to our negative deeds, whether from this life or past lives. True Source Love can even erase our negative karma from our past lives. However, we need to open our heart to accept True Source Love and be willing to change our attitude, habits and mistakes. It is best for us to admit the wrongdoings that we are aware of having done, then be remorseful and ask for forgiveness. True Source is always loving us, but by admitting, being remorseful and asking for forgiveness, the parts of us that made the mistake can be opened to accept the most beautiful blessing from True Source.

Opening our heart completely to True Source so we can accept True Source Love completely will change our lives. As I have mentioned previously, that is True Source Will. So, how can we experience it? Let us do the following experiments (don't forget, use your heart with your inner heart as director):

- Pray to True Source so **our heart is opened completely to True Source**
- Pray to True Source so that **we can surrender all hopes related to our heart to True Source** so that whatever True Source Will may be on our heart can happen completely.

For those of you who have used your heart and inner heart as director, you will be able to feel a very big difference between the two points above when we are praying to True Source. Haven't we realized that praying is only a facility to prioritize True Source to accept True Source Love?

Why do we need to pray so True Source can open our hearts

completely to True Source (refer to the first point above)? Even when we are in prayer, we will have an interest in the benefits that we will receive, so it is undeniable that a part of our heart is:

- Taking care of our own interests, in this case our own heart (to be able to be opened to True Source)
- Taking care so in the prayer, we can receive the results that we hope for

We need to underline that opening our heart to True Source completely is not simply a desire of our true self, but much more, it is True Source Will. Nevertheless, in opening our heart, we will unconsciously still have these interests, because we need True Source in addition to our own personal interests.

Our heart will be used to take care of at least the two points I mentioned above. Whatever our prayer may be, whatever we may need, this will still occur.

However good our heart attitude may be when we pray to True Source, our heart will not prioritize True Source completely. Our heart will tend to put our own needs, interests and desires first. So, how do we, with all of our weaknesses, improve this particular weakness so we are more wholehearted in prioritizing True Source? As we have discussed in **Chapter 13** this journey, this life is not about becoming a perfect being, but to always let ourselves be loved and helped by True Source.

As soon as we are aware that we need to pray for True Source to open our heart completely to True Source, a part of our heart will automatically be occupied in taking care of that matter. Therefore, we need to begin our prayer to True Source by surrendering our interest in those matters that we need help with. As we do so, True Source Love will be able to help the parts of our heart that are still occupied with our needs, interests and desires, so they can be freed from those matters and our heart can prioritize True Source more completely.

You may think that my discussion sound like I'm playing mind games with True Source. But this is certainly not the case. Even before we pray, True Source already knows what's within our deepest thoughts and feelings. Hence, it is impossible to deceive True Source. In praying, what is really important is our willingness to prioritize True Source. This is a part of an important realization; we are full of weaknesses and only with the help of True Source Love can we improve our weaknesses.

For a deeper understanding, remember that there is a very deep and hidden part within our spirit which left True Source, and which refused to be loved. Those parts that left True Source and refused to be loved by True Source, left for no other reason than prioritizing their own needs, interests and desires.

When we are willing to be helped by True Source Love in surrendering our needs, interests and desires in everything that we go through, then at the same time:

- Our whole heart will prioritize True Source more and more
- Our whole heart will be able to accept True Source Love that True Source has already bestowed upon us, for us to obtain a better result
- Parts within our spirit that are still refusing to return completely to True Source are being surrendered to True Source

These are the moments when we use what we go through in life as a facility to choose and prioritize True Source.

2. Just to be Loved by True Source

If we start our prayer by surrendering our needs, interests and desires, it will make us more wholehearted in prioritizing True Source. Those parts of our heart previously occupied with our personal needs, interests and desires will "change course" to instead prioritize True Source. However, this does not mean that our heart is already completely for True Source. Our relationship with True Source is very deep and in this regard, I would like to take the opportunity to discuss another important step to help us improve our heart attitude to True Source.

Starting our prayer with surrendering our needs/ interests/desires will make us more wholehearted in prioritizing True Source.

Let us now try, with your whole heart and inner heart as director, to do the following:

- **Pray to True Source so all of our hopes related to our heart can be surrendered to True Source**, so whatever True Source Will in relation to our heart can happen completely.

- **Pray to True Source only to be loved by True Source**, so whatever True Source Will in relation to our heart can happen completely.

The second point above is another important step that will improve our heart attitude to True Source. In a similar way to when we are surrendering our needs, interests and desires, all we need to do is pray to True Source with our heart and inner heart as director. True Source always gives us the best. As soon as we pray with our heart and inner heart as director, willing to be helped by True Source Love, then True Source Love will immediately help us. All we need to add after we surrender our needs, interests and desires is to pray only to be loved by True Source. As we do so, our heart attitude will be towards True Source.

Perhaps you are silently asking: but doesn't the previous discussion say that by surrendering our needs, interests and desires to True Source, our heart is prioritizing True Source more? What is the connection between praying to be loved by True Source and surrendering to True Source? This is a good question. I will explain the answer in the simplest way possible. By surrendering our needs, interests and desires, our whole heart is prioritizing True Source more and is more directed towards True Source, but our heart is not yet accepting True Source Love. After we let True Source Love help us in praying just to be loved by True Source, then our heart will prioritize True Source even more, and henceforth will feel like there is nothing to lose, which spiritually speaking, is a part of surrendering to True Source.

If you are unsure about how to pray to True Source for the matters that we have discussed, here are a couple of examples that will hopefully help you. You are free to use your own wordings and do not have to follow it word by word.

Prayer before Studying

True Source, we are so grateful to You because You love us completely every single moment.

True Source, please help us to surrender all hopes/desires/interests in studying and in everything else, so that this moment, when we are praying to You and afterwards when we are studying, to just to be loved by You.

True Source, please help us to realize that Your Will is the most Beautiful for us and please help us so that we can study properly just according to Your Will.

Thank You, True Source...
Amen.

Prayer before Working

True Source, we are so grateful to You because You love us completely every single moment.

True Source, please help us to surrender all hopes/desires/interests in working and in everything else, so that this moment, when we are praying to You and afterwards when we are working, to just to be loved by You.

True Source, please help us to realize that Your Will is the most Beautiful for us and please help us so that we can work properly just according to Your Will

Thank You, True Source...
Amen.

Chapter 16
Sixth Key: Using Every Moment in Life to Choose True Source

Many people assume that to choose True Source completely means that we must leave behind our worldly life: leaving behind work, family and everything else to meditate in solitary caves at the slopes of some remote mountain or at least to dwell in a special place away from all worldly distractions to be able to choose True Source completely. This assumption is definitely incorrect. Remember that returning to True Source is True Source Will - not just for one group of beings but for every being, including you and me.

Fundamentally speaking, we humans were created as social beings that need to interact with each other. It is through our interaction with others that the weaknesses within our spirit can surface automatically and easily. As a human, our physical body, feelings, thoughts etc. are designed especially by True Source in such a way that all of the weaknesses within our spirit can surface easily. Our best and most valuable moments are when we interact with others, when we want or need something, when we have problems and so on. Imagine if we needed to meditate for 10 years just to find one of our weaknesses, while in fact we still have an abundance of weaknesses within us.

So that we can use every moment of our lives to choose True Source completely, we will discuss the following matters:

- Our daily life is the true spiritual journey
- Choosing True Source means leaving behind the "old us"
- Choosing True Source when problems/needs arise
- Being grateful to True Source in good times
- Being loved by True Source every moment
- Why do problems still exist?
- Everything as an offering of Love for True Source
- Choosing and prioritizing True Source must become a part of our life

A. Our Daily Life is the True Spiritual Journey

Many people may be unaware of an important matter about our spiritual journey and the way it relates to the true purpose of our life: our daily life is our true spiritual journey. People assume that interacting and socializing with others will make us busy or take us away from calmness, preventing our spiritual life from advancing. This is definitely a misconception. Doing unnecessary things does make us busy. So, do not be involved in unnecessary things. However, working and taking care of your business, family, everything else are integral parts of our spiritual lessons. Everything has been chosen and planned specifically for us, to help us with all of our weaknesses.

Our heart is the main and most important key. Our heart is the key connection with True Source. Only by opening our heart to True Source can we receive True Source Love that will also instantly give many positive benefits to our heart and spirit. So, when should we open our heart for True Source? Only when we are praying? Do we need to leave behind our lives and daily responsibilities to be able to open our heart continuously to True Source? The answer is "No". We neither need to, nor should we leave behind our lives and our daily responsibilities. When we are faced with life and our daily responsibilities, we are being given a chance to choose True Source. If we prioritize and open our heart to True Source at those moments when we are busy with our responsibilities and our worldly needs, we will advance. At those moments, we are choosing True Source more than ourselves. (Please refer to the book **The Real You: Beyond Forms and Lives**).

After we begin to realize more of our own journey from our previous lifetimes, we will appreciate that where our family is born, our body shape and so on are not simply coincidences. Everything is very much related to our past life journey. That is the reason some babies are born on a very soft and beautiful bed, while others are born on an old carpet in a shabby hut. Although both have just been born on earth, what each of them did in their previous life affected their current condition. Our current condition, that is our daily life, is the best facility for our spiritual journey to choose True Source

Our daily life is our true spiritual journey

In our daily life we have the beautiful opportunity to choose True Source. From the moment we wake up, what will we do first? Do we attend to our business and interests or do we remember True Source and be grateful to True Source for all the beautiful blessings that we have received and are still continuously receiving every moment? If we use the morning for our interests, whether we are doing normal routine things or very important matters, everything is still "for us" or "our interests". We certainly still need to take care of our responsibilities. However, in doing so, are we prioritizing True Source and True Source Love? This is what I mean by choosing True Source; this is our spiritual journey. These are beautiful moments when we can change our everyday matters (from a human perspective) into special and beautiful moments when we choose True Source.

No matter whether you are a housewife, a student, an employee, an executive, an official or even an elderly retiree, everything that you go through and you do throughout the day is an opportunity to choose True Source. The moments when we choose True Source more than our own interests are the moments that we are advancing spiritually provided that we are choosing True Source without abandoning our worldly duties and responsibilities.

Situations often arise when it seems like whatever we are concentrating on requires our whole time, attention and commitment so that we cannot prioritize True Source. This example shows that there are parts within us that have not yet prioritized True Source completely. Why do I say this? If you have similar thoughts to the one mentioned above, it is an indication that:

- We forget that our whole life and every moment is a facility to prioritize True Source

167

- We are still working or doing whatever we do just for our interests
- We still feel that we can do those things better than if we are helped by True Source Love
- We forget that True Source is the Source of Prosperity

In those situations, we need to remember the true purpose of our lives and that we can only do the best when True Source Love is helping us. This means the best not only for the true purpose of our lives but also in the worldly tasks that we are encountering. Whether it is to achieve a result, get a promotion, for our fortune, or for absolutely everything else, only True Source can give us the best.

Sometimes, we even fool ourselves. We often fool ourselves into thinking that in living our lives, we have prioritized and chosen True Source. Yet, it is still only in our thoughts. Our heart is not yet doing so properly. We need to realize this because the extent to which we choose and prioritize True Source is not to gain a score or for our pride. It is truly for our everlasting relationship with True Source, which is the main purpose of our lives. So, how can we improve those two conditions?

After putting into practice the important keys from previous discussions, one of the very important elements in our relationship with True Source is being grateful to True Source. That is why I will include this as the "seventh key" which will be discussed exclusively in the next chapter.

B. Choosing True Source Means Leaving Behind the "Old Us"

After opening our heart better to True Source, we are actually gradually leaving behind the "old us", our ways, attitudes, habits and so on. Our negative emotions are reduced, we are now calmer, more peaceful, remembering and prioritizing True Source more and performing our worldly duties and responsibilities as an offering of Love for True Source. The longing from within our heart for True Source is also clearer, so that we begin to need special time to pray and enjoy True Source Love for us.

We can say that we are beginning to choose True Source more properly after we start putting into practice the five important keys that we have discussed. As we do so, our necessary learning will often change. For example, family members will begin to interact better with each other, or we may receive different opportunities at work. Yet we will still often feel that there are old habits, ways, attitudes or some things within us that are still not the best even though we have improved and are closer to True Source. These are the chances to surrender all of these matters to be closer to True Source.

By doing this, we are choosing True Source. We know that sometimes our old habits, ways, attitudes and so on that are not the best can surface a lot more easily with those who we are closer to, rather than those we are not so close to. The people closest to us are our facilities who help us in cleansing everything that is not the best, because all of these things originate from our spirit. If we were to remove ourselves from people and hide ourselves away, we would not have any interaction with others in those moments. We may feel calm and peaceful but this means that the weaknesses originating from our spirit are still within us and are not surfacing; hence it will be harder to take care of those weaknesses. Without letting True Source Love help us with our weaknesses, even though those weaknesses do not increase, they do not reduce or disappear as they are simply repressed.

Remember that our life is not a coincidence, instead it is a gift of Love from True Source, personally given to each of us to help our spirit in choosing True Source. True Source has chosen the best for each and every one, including the roles that we face, everything that we go through, our condition and so on. It is time to realize this, to be grateful to True Source and to start using our life according to True Source's beautiful plan, which is for us to choose True Source, so that our true self and our spirit, can return to True Source to be joyful with True Source forever and ever.

Sometimes we experience that we have chosen True Source quite well, but the people around us are not yet able to choose True Source in the same way we choose True Source. We cannot force this situation. We can just do our best and pray while surrendering the results to True Source. This is in fact a beautiful opportunity for us to help them *(especially those who are closest to us such as our own family)* to prioritize True Source more and more.

I notice that many people have the wrong understanding about this matter. They feel that because they have opened their hearts and have prayed diligently, their lessons have been completed. The easiest way to recognize this is to look at all your situations. Are we still influenced or reacting negatively? If the answer is "YES", then it means that we still need to be more wholehearted in choosing True Source. Usually those who feel that they are spiritually very advanced are the ones who still need to improve a lot.

C. Choosing True Source when Problems/Needs Arise

As we have previously discussed, it is True Source Will for us to remember True Source, and to remember True Source Unlimited Love for us so that when our needs or problems arise, we will use those moments to open our heart to True Source. We will then use those moments to surrender our desires, interests and problems to prioritize True Source more completely.

Problems and needs are not to be ignored or abandoned, because the situation will not change by itself. If we try to take care of those matters on our own, we may get a positive result, but we will not become closer to True Source. Only when we use moments and opportunities like these to choose True Source, are we using our lives and what we go through, as a facility to remember and direct our heart to True Source. First we must have surrendered our hopes, needs and problems when we pray and then we just do our best. We pray to be able to let ourselves be freed from our worries and busyness and be willing to be loved by True Source. When these happen together then, at the same time, we are also surrendering everything that is not the best within our spirit that has been there since before our very first incarnation.

D. Being Grateful to True Source in Good Times

When something positive happens to us, for example moving to a new home or during happy times, such as birthdays, what are we feeling or doing? Are we just being joyful, happy and enjoying everything? Often we may feel we are but unfortunately, spiritually speaking, we are wasting those beautiful moments. Why? Because we are not using those beautiful moments to be closer to True Source. We forget and are lulled into not remembering True Source. By being grateful to True Source with our heart and inner heart as director, we can realize and admit that the beautiful things that we receive, or the joyful moments we experience are True Source gifts of Love for us.

Only when we are being grateful to True Source with our heart and inner heart are we using good moments and opportunities as a facility to be closer to True Source. By being grateful to True Source, realizing and admitting that those beautiful moments are purely True Source Gifts of Love for us, then our heart will be more directed towards True Source. Our heart will also automatically surrender more completely to True Source, because we have admitted how those good things originated from True Source. Our heart will be able to prioritize True Source and accept True Source gifts of Love more completely. On the other hand, without gratitude to True Source, although we feel happy, joyful and are able to enjoy those good moments, our heart is still prioritizing our desires or habits. If we let this happen or even let this become a habit, our heart will realize less and less how True Source always loves us, how every good thing is a part of True Source Love for us, bringing True Source gifts of love for us.

E. Being Loved by True Source Every Moment

In times of need or when problems arise we should remember True Source, remember True Source Love, and pray with our whole heart and inner heart as director, to True Source to be helped with our needs and problems. It should be no different to when we are receiving or experiencing something good; those should be the moments we remember True Source. We should remember that it is only possible for all good things to be received and to happen to us because of True Source unlimited Love for us, and then to be grateful to True Source.

So, when should we remember and pray to True Source? The answer is simple: *every moment is the perfect time to remember and pray to True Source*. As we have previously discussed, even if we have needs and desires, we can let True Source Love help us in surrendering all of our problems, desires and wants to True Source. It will be even better if we ask for True Source's help by praying to True Source to just be loved by True Source. In moments when our heart attitude is to be loved by True Source, we (our spirit) reduces its busyness, prioritizes True Source and receives the best and the most beautiful gifts of love from True Source for eternity.

Even when we are not receiving or experiencing something good (when we are in trouble and have problems), or indeed when we are happy, we still need to be wholehearted and with our inner heart as director, so that we can let ourselves be loved by True Source every moment. Only then can such moments make our life more meaningful, which is by using it according to True Source Will. These are the moments when we let True Source Love help our spirit to be closer to True Source.

In these moments, our feelings, thoughts and whole selves are within the beauty of True Source Love. Not only will our feelings be filled with beautiful sensations and our mind be calmed, but it is also good for everyone around us; our environment.

Prayer to be loved by True Source (example)

True Source, we are so grateful to you because you love and take care of us completely every moment

True Source, please help us to surrender all of our hopes, desires, and interests to You, just to prioritize Your love for us, to be loved by You continuously without stopping, as the most beautiful and the most important thing for us

Thank You, True Source...

Amen

F. Why do Problems Still Exist?

If we have put the five points above into practice in our everyday lives, why does it sometimes still feel like problems will just never leave us? If you still encounter problems in your life, it means that you are still living a normal life, that you are still on earth. The more important question is now, how do we react towards those so-called "problems"?

Are we still reacting negatively to the incidents we label problems, whether related to our work, relationships, and so on?

Are we still using our old habits, ways and attitudes? If the answer is "yes", it means that the presence of those problems is reminding us of the "lesson" that we have not yet completed. We still doubt True Source's unstoppable Love. If we want to open our heart and allow True Source Love to help us, then True Source Love will really help us. In the most beautiful way True Source Love will cleanse our tainted selves of everything that is not the best and has surfaced from our spirit, irrespective of whether it has become a habit of our soul or brain.

That is why, if we still react negatively towards the problems that we face it simply means we are not yet letting True Source Love help us and we are not being loved by True Source properly enough. You may feel that what is happening to you is extraordinary and that you need to express negative emotions and so on. It is true that we must not abandon our responsibilities. For example, if we know someone is not doing the right thing, it is our responsibility to advise or help that person. However, giving advice and being emotionally reactive are two completely different things. Often, we are giving "advice" while being emotional and if we are truly honest, what comes out of our mouth is then not purely constructive advice. Instead, we express our own frustration and negative emotions. It is useless only to vent our own negative emotions. It is best to give advice without negative emotions, but within True Source Love. In those moments, True Source Love can touch and work in the best way possible on the people receiving our advice.

In relation to this matter, I would like to give an analogy. There is a class with a few dozen students and they are about to begin an important exam. As soon as they read the questions, some students begin to write down the answers while smiling. Other students start getting frustrated and grumbling as soon as they read the questions. When the time is up, the students who completed their exams complaining and grunting, still have a grumpy face when handing in their exam papers and leave the room while complaining about the paper, the school and so on.

Now let us take a closer look at the analogy above. Why are some students able to complete the exam properly, while others have difficulties or are even unable to complete the given questions? It is clear that those who completed the questions easily could do so because they had studied and prepared themselves appropriately, isn't it? It is most likely (or indeed certain) that those who were not able to complete their exam did not prepare themselves properly.

Would you agree that the students who were grumbling did not need to complain about so many things, including the school, the teacher, the curriculum, etc.? Isn't it clear that their inability to complete the exam should be the moment that helps them realize that they should have been better prepared and to study more properly from now on? Do not look for mistakes around you; find the fault within yourself instead, to correct it.

We need to start realizing from now on that our life is a facility for us to learn to choose and prioritize True Source, to help our spirit to prioritize True Source. I hope that the analogy of the students and the exam can be a subject of contemplation for all of us. We will always encounter problems in our lives. If we face them with a smile from our heart, because we feel that we are being loved by True Source, it means that we have prepared ourselves properly. On the other hand, if we are facing a certain situation or a problem and we still react negatively, it is only a beautiful facility to remind us that we have not yet prepared ourselves properly. We are not being loved by True Source properly, or to be exact. We have not let True Source Love fill our hearts, because we have not yet opened our hearts for True Source.

In addition, we are still living on earth where nothing is perfect. However, we must remember that it is in that very imperfection that the beautiful facilities have been provided for us, to use our life more in accordance with True Source Will. After all, this life and this world are not merely a means for manifesting our desires and ambitions.

In using our lives and everything we go through as a beautiful facility to choose and prioritize True Source, we can gradually feel everything becoming better, whether it is our job, career, work, relationships with our family and with others, health and so on. After all, True Source is also the Source of Prosperity, The True Healer and The Source of all that is most beautiful.

Do not look for mistakes around us,
find the fault within ourselves to correct it.

G. Everything as an Offering of Love for True Source

Everything we go through should only be used as a facility to choose and prioritize True Source. This applies to moments when we have desires, needs and problems as well as moments when we receive and experience something beautiful. Even in our everyday lives we should use every moment and opportunity to be loved by True Source, because everything will only be completed if we do our job and daily activities also as an offering of love for True Source.

Why is that? Because if not, there are two separate matters that we are busy attending to:

- Carrying out our activities/our duties
- Being loved by True Source

This will result in our heart not being directed completely to True Source. There are still parts of our heart that are being used to take care of our activities and duties for our desires. It is similar to surrendering our desires, needs and problems to True Source before we pray. By praying to True Source so that everything we do can be our offering of love to True Source, then the following important changes will happen:

- Our heart (spirit) will prioritize True Source more completely
- Our heart (spirit) will accept True Source Love more completely

Here are a few example prayers that you can use to surrender everything just as an offering of Love to True Source:[5]

Prayer before Studying

True Source, we are so grateful to You because You love us completely, every moment.

True Source, please help us to surrender all of our hopes/desires/needs in studying or in everything else so we can pray to You now and study afterwards, just to be loved by You more completely and just as our offering of love for You

True Source, please help us, as Your Will is the most beautiful for us, and please help us to be able to study properly just in accordance with Your Will.

Thank You, True Source. Amen

---

[5] The two example prayers are quite similar to previous prayers, indeed our lives is just to rely on True Source Love and to choose True Source more completely. The difference is that the two following prayers have a little addition so that what we do can just be our offering of love to True Source.

Prayer before Working

True Source, we are so grateful to You because You love us completely, every moment.

True Source, please help us to surrender all of our hopes/desires/needs in working or in everything else so we can pray to You now and work afterwards, just to be loved by You more completely and just as our offering of love for You

True Source, please help us as Your Will is the most beautiful for us, and please help us to be able to work properly just in accordance with Your Will.

Thank You, True Source. Amen

H. Choosing and Prioritizing True Source Must Become a Part of our Life

If we can put all of these realizations into practice properly then we will feel a tangible difference. However, often people will say, "How am I supposed to do all of this with all the busyness and responsibilities in my daily life?" If you are still concerned about this matter, ask yourself: "Why are you living your life?" Just to work for a living or to reach the true purpose of your life?

Of course we still need to work and carry out our duties and responsibilities properly. However, it is time for us to realize that by being helped by True Source Love, we can complete our duties and responsibilities

179

in the best way, not only for us, but also for others, and most importantly, in the best way in accordance to True Source Will. At the same time, while completing our duties and responsibilities, we are also fulfilling the true purpose of our lives in the best possible way, which is, by using the "true path" provided personally by True Source. Being loved by True Source and doing everything as an offering of Love for True Source does not mean we are wasting our time. A short prayer to be able to do things properly only takes a few minutes. We have many of those "few minutes" in our daily lives that we usually waste or use on other things.

From a worldly point of view, if we are willing to use a short few minutes to pray wholeheartedly–with our inner heart as director – to True Source, even when we are busy, our heart and mind will be calmer. We will be guided by True Source and will obtain ideas and solutions that we have never thought of. Yes, we will receive the best help.

Actually, from a spiritual point of view, there is a reason why we still look for excuses not to be loved by True Source completely and continuously and there is a reason why we are not living our life as an offering of love for True Source, even though we have directly felt the beauty of being loved by True Source. The reason is that there are still parts of us, or more accurately our old self, which likes our habits, attitudes, and ways and wants to keep it that way. All of this is within our spirit. If we still insist on nurturing those bad habits, it means that we are still holding on to those things that cause us not to be able to choose and prioritize True Source completely. We are already closer to True Source, but to really reach the true purpose of life, we must surrender *everything* completely. Only then can our whole heart and whole being choose and prioritize True Source. Only then can we be helped to receive the most beautiful gifts of Love that have been provided for us, to be together with True Source forever and ever.

Chapter 17
Seventh Key: Being Grateful to True Source Every Moment

We have previously talked about being grateful to True Source when times are good - when we receive or obtain something according to our hopes, or when we experience something beautiful. By being grateful to True Source at such moments, we are reminding ourselves that everything good is a part of True Source unlimited Love for us. Our heart will be more directed to True Source and will prioritize True Source Love for us.

However, only being grateful to True Source in good times is not enough. In addition to remembering True Source and remembering True Source unlimited love for us as well as prioritizing True Source Love all the time, we need to be grateful to True Source at *every moment*. You may be confused how we can be grateful to True Source at every moment. What if we are not receiving or experiencing good things all the time? This is where one of the important keys lies in the understanding of our spiritual journey that many people are unaware of.

In our daily lives, we are more fixated on our "agenda", which consists of our desires, interests and busyness. Even when we are doing this True Source still loves us continuously, but our lives, our heart and ourselves are within our "agenda". Regardless of how important we hold True Source Unlimited Love in our minds, the Love that is the best and the most beautiful for eternity, is in fact still separated from us. We know that everything in life is just temporary, including everything we do and our accomplishments.

However extraordinary our accomplishments may be, even if our names are written in human history, everything is still just temporary. What I am sharing with you is not based on mere theory, but is shown clearly by our heart attitude. It shows in how wholeheartedly we surrender everything to choose True Source and True Source Love for us. Further discussion about being grateful to True Source every moment can be read in the next book I am writing. Stay tuned!

With a heart that is always grateful to True Source, our heart will automatically be more directed towards, and prioritize True Source and True Source Love so that our heart will be even more filled with calmness, peacefulness and all the most beautiful things from True Source unlimited Love. Our mind will be calmer. Negative emotions that often surface such as jealousy, envy, dissatisfaction and so on will reduce drastically. We will no longer be busy with our desires that in the past seemed endless because we will better enjoy what we already have.

Nevertheless, some people feel worried and make the assumption that if they are too grateful they will be lazy or not have enough motivation to improve. I dare say to you that this is not correct. When we are really and properly more grateful to True Source, we will carry out our duties and responsibilities properly. The results of our work will be better due to the change in our attitude as we rely on True Source help more. Even in our spiritual advancement we will get the best because we are being guided and blessed by True Source.

Chapter 18
Eighth Key: Sharing True Source Love with All Beings

Sharing True Source Love is very important in order to become closer to True Source. How can we be grateful to True Source for True Source Love, especially to prioritize True Source Love, without understanding the meaning of love itself? When we are only thinking of our own needs and self, no matter how much we think we have chosen True Source, everything is just in our mind. It is not reflected in our heart attitude and actions, because it is still for our own interests.

We have extensively discussed surrendering all of our desires, and even our interests to True Source. However, this is not enough. We also need to share with others all the gifts of love from True Source that we have received. Some may be in the form of giving to charity and doing good deeds to others but this is just a part of it. So, how should we share True Source Love with all beings?

To share True Source Love, we need to be as True Source instruments.

To become True Source instruments, we need to surrender our whole heart and self to True Source to be used by True Source completely as a facility, so that True Source Love can work in the most beautiful way for all beings. Surrendering our whole heart and self to True Source to be used as instruments is a deeper surrendering to True Source. Our whole heart and self will be more completely within True Source Love and will open more and more completely towards True Source Love.

However much our heart is opened, if we do not share True Source Love with others, it will still be like a container with edges that limit True Source Love. Only by sharing True Source Love as True Source instruments for all beings can our heart and whole being be opened without limit, to be loved by True Source completely.

Chapter 19
Advice

If someone asks me about my spiritual level, I always answer that I simply opened my heart to True Source a little bit earlier than some of you. I am always reminding people that only True Source is the true teacher of every being. All other beings are True Source subjects who are also on their journey to return to True Source completely. Only when we remember this in our minds and actions, as well as relying on True Source Love in every moment, can we then remain on the right path to be closer to True Source forever. For that, we need to use our heart and inner heart properly.

Although I often discuss various things in the books that I write, everything is just to share my experiences. I always think of everyone who joins the workshops I teach as my friends who are on the same journey as me.

As I have taught and met many people from a wide variety of backgrounds, I have come to realize something interesting that I would like to share with those of you who belong to this category. Many people who have practiced and mastered different techniques for years have felt differences from the workshops that I have taught. Some even said that what they learnt in just two days during the workshop had surpassed what they have practiced for many years or even decades. However, they also feel like it is a pity to let go of what they have learnt and been practicing for many years.

This is an important matter that you need to realize after reading this book. If you are practicing a technique diligently and with commitment, you will for sure get results. However, is that result what you really want?

The analogy is: if we are in the middle of the island of Java and we have been walking towards the east so that one day we reach the easternmost point of Java then, the question arises, is the easternmost point of Java where you really wanted to go? If in fact you wanted to reach the northernmost point of Java, then you are walking the wrong way. You need to stop your journey as soon as possible and change direction to the proper one, the faster, the better.

Returning to our previous discussion, every technique or spiritual method has for sure its own benefits, especially if that benefit contributes to the good of others. However, if your purpose is to be closer to True Source, especially to return to True Source completely, then True Source Love is the only way. Hence, with all due respect, I would like to advise you to choose True Source as your only purpose with True Source Love as your path. If the path you have followed does not bring you to choose True Source completely, no matter how long you have practiced it, surrender and let it go because choosing True Source is the best and the most beautiful eternally. Believe it.

Chapter 20
Additional Information

A. Sharing

Below, you will find several personal sharings from our friends who have started to realize more about the true purpose of life.

My Journey to find True Love

After my mother passed away when I was small, I was raised by my grandmother. She was a teacher of the Al-Quran. It was with her that I learnt to read the Al-Quran in Arabic to completion (Khatam). I also learnt to do my prayers (Sholat) and fasted with Grandma. Grandma put me in a religious school and made me enjoy studying religion and listening to the lectures given in the mosques. Since I was small, I always asked within my heart, how come I still cannot understand the content of the Al-Quran that entails guidance for human life?

In my teenage years, I received an Al-Quran with translation. I felt so happy. Every time I finished reading the verses of the Al-Quran, I always read the meaning, until I read every single verse of the Al-Quran. Even though I finished reading the Al-Quran, I still did not understand, because I was only reading without realizing.

In 1960, my uncle invited me to live with him and my auntie in Jakarta until I got married. I continued to enjoy listening to the recitation of the Al-Quran. I desired more and more to comprehend the Al-Quran.

I am so grateful to Allah, in 1980, Allah granted me the wealth to complete my pilgrimage to the holy land of Mecca. In front of the Ka'bah, I always prayed: Allah, your subject wants to know the meaning behind the words of the Al-Quran. Allah, please open your secrets within the Al-Quran to your subject…

I prayed the same prayer for 40 days in front of the Ka'bah.

When I returned from Mecca, for years, I continued to search many places, looking for a teacher who could teach me the meaning of the Al-Quran to guide my life. Unfortunately, what I was looking for, I was still yet to find.

So I prayed again: Allah, wherever that teacher may be, whether beyond the ocean or in the furthest place, as long as you give me sufficient wealth for me to reach him/her, I will go, I will sacrifice all of my wealth and life according to your Will. Allah, please help your subject…

I continued to search without losing hope. Following in the footsteps of Moses looking for his teacher, Moses said, "I will not stop (walking) until I meet the teacher that I have been looking for, or I will continue to walk for years".

Meeting a Teacher

Around 1985, Allah blessed me to meet a teacher who taught me about understanding the Al-Quran, that is by: "The verse is explained by the verse in the Al-Quran". According to him, the Al-Quran consists of 6,666 verses. Similar to a stack of rattan wattle connected into a building; they are all interconnected (help each other) and he taught me in a language that I understood, Indonesian. In the beginning of the learning process, he asked me "What is your purpose in learning about the Al-Quran?" I answered, "So I can understand the fundamental principles of life". He then asked again, "Once you have achieved what you want, you will have the responsibility to share it with others." Then I said, "Yes, ustadz (term for a Muslim religious Teacher), I will share with others."

Knowing Myself

When I first learnt from that teacher, he asked me to read one of the Al-Quran's verse, that says: May you know that there is no God other than Allah.

After I read it, the teacher told me that the meaning is the literal understanding, and that the meaning within is: "That you have the responsibility to search for knowledge about Allah," he repeated. "Then go look for knowledge so that you know Allah", he added.

Mohammed the prophet once said: "Whoever knows himself will undoubtedly know His God." Because of that, the first lesson I was taught is to **"know myself"**: who am I? Where did I come from? Where am I now? And where am I going?

He taught me beginning with the realm of souls, then the realm of the womb, realm of earth, and at the end of life we will return through death's door, separation of body and spirit, doomsday, the place where humans congregate at doomsday, heaven, hell. Starting from the creation of the body until our spirit is blown into it. We are alive because of the union of the spirit and body. Someday, our spirit that is given vision, hearing and inner heart will return to Allah. So, during prayer, we meet with Allah. He also gave to me knowledge about Allah. Allah is the Infinite layers of Light. Allah is Love. Within us is a little part of that light and love.

We must be able to see Allah, we must meet again with Allah while still alive.

There is a verse in the Al-Quran that explains, those whose hearts are blind on earth; they will be even blinder and lost in the afterlife.

When my teacher succumbed to sickness due to old age, I asked him, do you have a friend who could teach me this? In return, he asked me, "Who bestowed the Al-Quran?" I answered, "Allah." He continued, "Then Allah should be your teacher."

Since the death of my teacher, my desire to meet Allah became stronger in my heart. I looked everywhere. I have met so many teachers, but what I wanted was to have knowledge about Allah, inner heart, spirit, soul; everything that is mentioned in the Al-Quran – I was yet to attain. I was also yet to find the practical method to connect my inner heart to the unlimited Source of Light.

At a certain time at night, I used to always find myself awake and asked Allah to help me meet someone who could teach me how to connect my inner heart with its Source. Because the Al-Quran teaches us that those who are devoted are those who can feel their connection with God.

Allah Listens to all Prayers

One day, I met someone who told me of a place where I can "open my heart", guided by a teacher by the name of Irmansyah Effendi. My heart was moved to learn. The lessons to open heart are given step by step, starting from level 1: the level of true self consciousness until more advanced levels, through the deepening of spiritual understanding.

Praise to Allah, the Most Holy, the All Loving and All Caring. Allah has granted my wish. During one of the events of deepening our spiritual understandings, I had the opportunity to chat with Mr. Effendi. He was so patient in listening to all my questions and in guiding me.

Feeling the Meeting with Allah

Through the lessons of opening heart, I have attended the true self consciousness program twice, I can start to feel and enjoy the beauty of praying, directing my face to Allah, especially when I say, "Wajjah- tu wajhiya lillazi fatarassamawati wal ardo hanifan musliman." Which means, I am directing my face to God who created the sky and the earth sincerely I surrender myself.

I am so grateful to Allah, that I have started to feel the beauty of the connection between the small nur (inner heart) and the Big Nur (Allah). Especially when I am sitting down, doing my tafakur, I can really feel how the light and love of Allah really flows and works beautifully within my heart and my whole body. Especially when I pray according to Mohammed's teaching: "Allah, please give light to my heart, give light to my hearing, give light to my vision, give light to my left, give light to my right, give light to my front, give light to my back, give light above me, give light below me, give light to my flesh and blood, give light to my hair and body."

Through these open heart lessons, I started to feel and realized that more and more meaningful and beautiful changes happen in my life. I started to feel the peacefulness, calmness and joy in my daily life with my family and friends. Gradually, the love and light of Allah that has filled my heart also erased the illnesses of the heart, such as arrogance, jealousy, showing off, vengeance, anger, ill-thoughts, being hypocritical, never satisfied, complaining, stingy, greedy, irritation, helplessness, etc.

Wherever I am, I started to feel the presence of Allah with me. Wherever I face, I can start to feel the beauty of all of Allah's creation around me. I can feel the beauty of nature, trees, leaves, grass, air, animals that I never realized before. I can also start to smile with joy and be grateful from the deepest part of my heart to God.

When I pray, I no longer ask for worldly matters, I only ask to be loved by Allah. I am so grateful to Allah, in facing the trials and tribulations of life, I start to realize how all of them are facilities to help me become closer to Allah. Through those facilities, I learn to surrender everything to Allah. I trust in the promise Allah made, that is whoever surrenders their lives to Allah always, Allah can bless them in unimaginable ways, Allah will ensure their needs are fulfilled and Allah will help in all of their matters.

I am so grateful to Allah for all the blessings of Love that have given me the opportunity to feel the beauty of being loved by Allah. Allah has given me this chance to open my heart because through my heart I can feel the presence of Allah through His Love. I feel that I have found what I have been looking for. And I am so thankful to my teacher, Mr. Effendi who has patiently guided me to The unlimited Love and Light of Allah.

FH

Knowing True Source

My name is Rida Fitara. I am a housewife and also a career woman. I am Buddhist. When I was small, I associated God with deities because I was influenced by my parents' beliefs. When I grew up and was much older, after going through a myriad of life's trials and tribulations, after getting bored with this and that, life started to feel empty and boring. I started to realize that going to the temple, filial piety, and taking care of the endless problems at work is not enough.

When I started to "search" – I tried to learn about Buddha Dharma – I felt it is in line with Buddha's teachings. When I felt ready to deepen my spiritual understanding, I came across Padmacahaya Foundation. At that time I became interested when I read the book **"Inner Heart"**.

It was at Padmacahaya where I started to realize, while being given guidance by the Teacher, that the true God is the Source of Eternal Love and Light, the only one who can bring us back to Him.

Since opening my heart, my relationship with True Source became better and better. By practicing diligently and following the workshops according to the curriculum, I realized more and more that True Source really loves us all so completely. Without asking, True Source has given us more than we need. It is so incredible.

My relationships with others also became more ideal. In the past, I often felt pity for those who I assumed were in a difficult situation. However, it turned out that I was not helping them be independent instead they became dependent on me. After opening my heart, I became more selective, I could sort out those who needed help according to True Source Will. The result is extraordinary, beyond my comprehension. I trust more and more that True Source is the All Knowing, Wisest beyond All, All Loving, All Everything. Now I no longer need to be burdened by unnecessary matters.

Every day I feel joyful and there are no more excuses not to be joyful. The beauty of True Source Love fulfills all the emptiness I was carrying within all this time. In working, I no longer need to be emotional, stressed etc. I used to consider that as normal. I am also more patient in facing competition. The result is beyond imagination. Without having to work extremely hard my business runs smoothly, even loans that I thought would never be recovered were paid back without having to harass anyone. It is so incredible.

After I realized the end purpose is to return to True Source, spirituality is no longer about chasing after what we want, but a facility to be closer to True Source, a facility to return to True Source completely according to True Source Will.

Now I see religion as a preliminary facility to know True Source on the surface. As a being with a brain and conscience, for sure we should not waste anything that our religion has taught us for so long. I continue to respect, love according to True Source Will, because it was not the religion that was lacking, but it was I, who did not open my heart enough to True Source – perhaps it was not time yet.

I am so lucky to join Guru Irman who constantly reminds us to prioritize True Source always, to trust and surrender everything including all of our problems to True Source, so that life feels more comfortable, peaceful, joyful, just being grateful to True Source every second.

I am so grateful and joyful to be able to be True Source instrument:

Sharing His Love and Light to all beings, helping every one of True Source beings and creations to return to True Source.

Oh, True Source, thank You for all of Your beautiful blessings. You are the Almighty. We are so grateful to You True Source, for all the abundant blessings to all of us. Please let Your Love help us so we can all love You and prioritize You in everything continuously, eternally.

Thank You, True Source. Thank you, Guru.

Rida Fitara

The Meaning of Spiritual Journey for Me

I am so grateful to True Source, the All Loving for His unlimited Love for all beings in the whole existence. Thank you to Mr. Irmansyah Effendi M.Sc. who has guided me and thousands of other Padmajaya/Padmacahaya alumni to realize the meaning of the real spiritual journey and to enjoy this life as a part of the spiritual journey that is so beautiful to experience. Please find my sharing below about the meaning of spiritual journey for me after learning to open my heart to True Source and True Source Love.

In this lifetime, I was born as a Balinese and my religion is Hindu, so my concepts and knowledge about karma, soul, atman/spirit, are quite complete. According to the understanding of my religion, the true purpose of life is to reach moksha or yoga, which is union with the Creator who is far above us. I once thought of becoming a yogi and meditating to cleanse my karma and practicing to reach yoga; however, with the busyness of the modern lifestyle, it seemed impossible to do.

I used to follow a spiritual organization that is led by a very famous teacher from India. He had millions of followers/students all over the world. He could create a lot of miracles, starting from healing various illnesses, creating something from thin air, as well as knowing about someone's future. I was actively involved with the social activities of that organization for 15 years, in Indonesia as well as in Australia when I completed my Masters. The humanitarian programs that I joined from those organizations such as helping the poor, providing food and aid for those who need etc. made me feel like I had completed my duties to others as taught in my religion. The spiritual programs that were taught such as meditation and other weekly practices as well as the ceremonies from the Hindu tradition made me feel that I was on my spiritual journey to become closer to True Source. In other words, I felt like I had completed the duties of my religion to become closer to True Source.

In 1998, I started to be acquainted with Reiki Tummo and then I also learned about opening heart to True Source and True Source Love from Mr. Irmansyah Effendi M.Sc. through the programs of Padmajaya Foundation. I started to realize more and more the meaning of the true spiritual journey. Before I knew and practiced opening my heart to True Source and True Source Love, I felt like I was already a good person, because I often helped others, meditated and prayed, and completed the religious ceremonies to become closer to True Source according to my religion. Evidently, after opening my heart, I only started to realize that all this time, my heart was still polluted with negative emotions, such as anger, vengeance, jealousy, arrogance and so on. I began to realize that I could not be close to True Source if my heart was still filled with negative emotions causing my spirit/atman/true self within my heart to become smaller, dimmer and further from True Source. By using my heart and inner heart as director, I could clearly feel how far my spirit was from True Source before I knew about opening heart to True Source and True Source Love and before letting True Source Love help to cleanse my heart.

The real changes in my life started to happen after I became more diligent in practicing the lessons about opening heart to True Source and True Source Love. My relationship with True Source became more beautiful and deeper. In addition, my relationship with others, my relationship with my wife and child also changed in quality. When doing good deeds for others, if our heart is not opened to True Source and filled with True Source love, these deeds alone will not touch our heart. I realized more and more that the real spiritual journey cannot be completed without the help of True Source Love through our heart that is opened to True Source Love. The spiritual journey that I thought was so difficult and long, filled with suffering, changed into something very beautiful as True Source Blessing to be enjoyed and walked with gratitude to True Source.

After joining the more advanced programs, I began to realize as a true essence more about the true relationship between our true self/atman/ spirit and True Source, the Source of every being's true self. Then the meaning of the real spiritual journey, our real purpose of life and our existence as a human on earth becomes clearer. I realize more and more how our spiritual journey is the journey of our spirit/ atman/true self in our heart to become closer to True Source. When we open our heart to True Source and True Source Love, our spirit/atman/ true self in our heart also grows/develops and the spiritual lessons that we learn as humans on earth also become easier to understand and go through. This means that at the same time, we are opening our heart to True Source and True Source Love, sharing the Love to others while interacting as humans, so that our spirit/atman/true self within our heart can also experience spiritual advancement, expand and become closer to True Source. This is neither difficult nor full of suffering, but rather it is so beautiful to experience.

Yes, we do not need to go to a holy place far away or become a hermit. Whoever we are, whatever we are, wherever we are it is sufficient (done in the proper way), to open our heart and embrace True Source Love and let True Source Love do everything needed on our whole heart and selves. Then True Source Love can cleanse our true self and everything that is not the best, including our negative karma, and bring our true self closer to True Source every moment. This beautiful realization shared by Mr. Irmansyah Effendi M.Sc has been experienced by thousands of practitioners around the world, fundamentally changing the meaning and purpose of the real spiritual journey. By realizing and experiencing directly as your true self, it is very clear that True Source really loves and cares for every being, and always helps every being to become closer to True Source. Even True Source Love helps us directly to bring us closer to True Source, without us needing to go somewhere special. I can feel so clearly, from the deepest part of my heart, that the spiritual journey of returning to True Source, is the destiny of every human. It is the Will of True Source for us.

I express my appreciation and gratitude to True Source who has brought me to meet Mr. Irmansyah Effendi M.Sc so that I can understand the meaning of the real spiritual journey. I do not need to use any of my own concepts/ideas or wants/wills to be closer to True Source because everything has been prepared and designed by True Source, The Creator in the best and most perfect way and so full of Love, a long time before I was born. We only need to be willing to be helped, cared for and loved by True Source completely. Infinite thanks to Mr. Irmansyah Effendi M.Sc and all of my spiritual siblings for all the help, prayers and love so that we can help each other so everyone can return to True Source completely.

Rama

Spiritual Seeker

I became an ardent spiritual seeker about forty years ago and my journey took me on many explorations searching for the truth of why we exist, the purpose of life and how to fulfill it. While engaging in different meditation disciplines for multiple hours, I thought I knew what it meant to follow my heart. While engaging in different spiritual pursuits, I was under the illusion that I was following a path that would lead to an advanced state of spiritual evolution. It was not until I became introduced to Irmansyah Effendi and the Padmacahaya Foundation curriculum, that I began to have my spiritual questions answered. These answers were not just something to fulfill my intellectual curiosity or my mind's wanting to know something more. These answers were realizations that came from the core of my being, and continue to ring so true and real. Previously, I did not realize the difference between soul and true self, and I thought that reaching a higher dimension was the appropriate direction to seek. Without a proper understanding of the difference between soul and true self (spirit), we may end up following a very limited path under the illusion that soul development is the same as spiritual growth. I

201

thought that spiritual fulfillment was directly related to "me" being in charge of my spiritual achievement and did not realize the Source of unconditional Love is waiting to give us the best of the best, beyond whatever I could possibly achieve by my doing. If you have been practicing meditation of any type, with the understanding that it is up to us to get to a "better place", then this book may be challenging to your paradigm. If this is what you are feeling, I understand because of the way I approached my spiritual journey for so many years. I would like to assure you that what you are reading in this book is not just a theory, but something that you can experience for yourselves. We can experience a spiritual transformation beyond what our mind may have even deemed possible and this can have a positive impact on every aspect of our life as we begin to experience profound gratitude to the Source of unconditional Love for mundane events or even the smallest of things.

Ed Rubenstein, Ph.d Psychologist

Spiritual Journey

As far as I remember, when I was in primary school I enjoyed the Hindu religious activities. I liked to pray and even to fast during certain days and I even invited and coordinated my friends to pray diligently and conduct religious ceremonies.

Everything went as normal until I became an adult and started my own family. All this time I felt that my understanding about religion and what is taught by my religion was very good. Every time I finished praying I felt calmer, happier and life continued normally. Every time there was a problem I prayed to the Creator, I felt comfortable and peaceful and I could convey anything that I experienced and felt to the Creator so that afterwards I would feel calm and joyful. At that time, for my standard it was more than enough. But there was one thing that didn't feel right in my heart. My religion teaches me that the purpose of life, that is attained after death, is moksha and to return to the Creator completely. However, I did not find the way to reach moksha and I thought only priests/ religious leaders or holy people could return to the Creator completely.

For sure it would have to be through a very long and continuous meditation. As I am just a normal person, how could it be possible? What is the way? My understanding of religion is also minimal, mainly continuing the rituals that were passed down from generation to generation and the religious studies at school. That was the biggest question mark that I felt, but I thought by doing what I had been taught by my religion it should be enough, even though I did not know where I would end up. I just did my best, until I attended a Reiki Tummo workshop, which I joined after fighting through various battles within myself. I asked myself, why would I want to learn something else if all the teachings of my religion are already more than enough?

Even though I felt a lot of inner disagreement, I could also feel something different; every time I practiced what was recommended in the workshop, I felt something else: calmness, peacefulness and other kinds of joy that I have never felt before. The more diligently I practiced, the more clearly I could feel everything until I could feel the beauty, longing and love that is so tangible from True Source.

When I attended the spiritual retreat level, it was explained that it is the destiny of every being to return to True Source. Ahaaa...! I then started to have the hope that ordinary people like me can also achieve the ultimate destiny as taught in my religion. The way and path to reach the destination is also explained in a crystal clear manner, that is by opening our heart completely to True Source. Encouraged by my strong curiosity, I then joined the "Open Heart Workshops". From here my heart became more and more certain that I could now feel and experience for myself everything that were formerly merely stories; the key is by opening our heart. I then started to choose to follow my heart. Then I decided to continue to the more advanced level until I attended the True Self Retreat. There, I was able to experience my spirit/true essence consciousness while still being alive on earth. It is incredible...I really could not imagine I had the chance to experience all of this...and it is all so real.

Now I can feel the real spiritual journey, when I pray my feeling becomes more beautiful, joyful, I feel so close to True Source and there is always a longing to make time to be connected to True Source.

The path to return to True Source feels so clear and direct. It turns out that True Source has been waiting for me to come home to True Source. All this time I never knew. I assumed that whatever I had learned, as long as I did it well enough would be sufficient for my afterlife. In reality, it is nowhere near. I can feel and experience this realization so clearly not only for myself, but actually for all other beings because True Source equally loves all beings and it is True Source Will for all beings to return to True Source. When I realize this, my heart expands without limit, so beautifully and joyfully. I am so grateful to True Source because I can realize and feel all of this. When I am in True Source Love and feeling the beauty, the joy of being loved by True Source and being able to share the Love as True Source instrument, it feels so much more tangible, even compared to all the physical things that are only temporary. Everywhere there is only love that is so gentle, feels so safe and comforting to be within…and I am supposed to be within the Love continuously because that is what my heart has been looking and longing for. It is so beautiful and I am so grateful to be able to feel and start to realize about this matter.

Layer by layer, my heart opens more and more, the Love feels clearer and the true joy starts to emerge and be freed so beautifully.

It turns out that all this time everything has been confined so deeply within the heart and covered with limitations and walls that I created myself. However, when my heart is open, everything feels so free and so beautiful. When True Source Love touches the deepest part of myself, there is a part of me that has been waiting for something. I am half in disbelief, what else am I waiting for? Isn't True Source Love the one my heart has been looking for and has now been found? Only when the part that has been waiting is touched, does everything open. It turns out, to return to True Source completely, I do not need to go anywhere, because The Creator Himself has come down to Earth and has come to give salvation to me and all beings through His parts. I have heard of stories about the parts of True Source who incarnate on Earth several times. Only when the last part incarnates, then everything is completed. When my heart realized that, my heart reacted so beautifully so much love and joy, so beautiful. So, the deepest part of me that has been waiting has been waiting for the arrival of the last part of True Source. That will complete everything True Source has planned through His parts that have previously incarnated as the key to open everything. If I use my brain, it seems near impossible or even preposterous because our brain is limited and temporary. Because of this limitation it can only understand limited and temporary matters. Only our inner heart, which is the spark of True Source within the heart that has been opened, can realize this unlimited divine matter. I feel that even my gratitude is not enough to express my appreciation because I can realize all of this by feeling and experiencing it directly.

True Source loves me so much that His Own part came down to Earth to give me salvation. That is why I have been born on this earth: because True Source knew that we could not find him. Try to think, where can we find True Source, with what, how? But True Source is the All Knowing and Almighty. Because of His unlimited and abundant Love, True Source Himself, through His Own parts, came down to look for me. All I have to do is just be willing to accept the presence of the final part of True Source, who came down to look for me, and be willing to be brought to wherever, in order to be with Him forever and ever. Even for this, True Source has organized and designed everything in the most beautiful way. Everything can be realized and experienced once my heart, inner heart, and the spark of True Source within me have been opened, freed and no longer imprisoned inside.

It was then that everything looked very bright, clear, and very real–no more secrets, no more doubts. Yes, I choose to trust my inner Heart, the spark of True Source within me because that is what the Creator wants.

The Creator placed the Creator's spark in the deepest part of my heart so that when my heart is open enough, I can realize, choose and follow what the Creator wants me to follow: the true truth from within my own heart. I no longer have to follow stories from other people. I feel very relieved, very free, very joyful, and very grateful to the Creator, and I realize that even this is only a fraction of what I still need to realize. I know that there are many Gifts of Love from the Creator I have yet to accept, as there is abundance and unlimited Blessings from the Creator.

Even with my limited realization, I have experienced significant changes in my daily life. I feel so much beautiful Divine Love every time I smile to or interact with others; I appreciate others better, and I don't feel superior to others. When I am able to invite others more directly to open their hearts to the Creator, my joy and gratitude to the Creator is even freer and more real. This is especially so when I witness my friends, who initially had difficulty smiling because they were burdened with problems and negative emotions, smile joyfully at the end of the Open Heart workshop. When they continued on to the next level all the way to realizing their true selves, I became even more grateful to the Creator because the Creator guides, helps, and directs each of them patiently and lovingly. It feels so beautiful and I'm so grateful. A true joy that can not be compared to anything else.

My relationship with my family members has also improved: we are now warmer towards one another and we are now more joyful. Although problems continue to exist, we are able to deal with them very differently now. I face all adversities in life now relying on True Source Love. Even prosperity comes to me without trying too hard to get what I want. It feels like True Source has organized everything so beautifully. The more we open our heart to the Creator, letting our- selves be loved and taken care of by the Creator, surrendering to the Creator, letting the Creator take care of everything, the more beautiful and meaningful life becomes. I no longer have to search high and low or go here and there because this earth is now just like the highest place I would have looked for in the past to find True Source. This is because True Source, through His Part is always with me on this Earth and being together with True Source is the true and eternal joy. I am so grateful to True Source. Thank you also to Mr. Irmansyah Effendi who is always guiding, directing, loving me so sincerely, patiently continuously even though sometimes I keep my distance. I am always reminded to return, continuously. Thank you to everyone for this beautiful togetherness as one heart for True Source, for True Source's beautiful plan for all beings: to return completely to True Source.

Ni Nengah Sumiarthi,

Jakarta

B. Spirituality Programs in Natural Way of Living

Using our lives in the best way possible for the true purpose of life is very important and beautiful. However, because our whole life is meant for that, it is not something we can take lightly or complete in a few months. Yet, it is something that can be done by anyone, whatever your profession may be, whether you are a student, a house wife, an employee, a business owner and so on.

You can look at the flow chart to get an understanding of the flow of workshops that I have designed at a glance. These workshops are for those who are interested in spiritual lessons, whether it is to simply know more, or to wholeheartedly achieve the true purpose of life. All the workshops in this flow chart are held by Padmacahaya.

Please be reminded that even though I refer to the "true purpose of life" in relation to the flow of spiritual programs by Padmacahaya, it does not mean that this is the absolute way to reach the true purpose of life. In reality the true purpose of life, to return to True Source, is the Gift of Love from True Source for every one of True Source sparks. But please do not forget that the key to our connection with True Source, whatever our form may be, wherever we are, is our heart. Without using our heart properly, our direct connection with True Source will be very limited. The best is of course to open and use our heart and inner heart as director, trusting and surrendering to True Source and using everything we go through in life just to choose True Source more and more completely.

Back to the spiritual program at Padmacahaya, there are two paths that you can choose from to begin: the Reiki Tummo path® and the Open Heart path. Even though both begin with opening, cleansing and strengthening the heart, the Reiki Tummo path also equips you with the ability to channel divine energy for your own and other's physical, mental and emotional health (for further information, you can refer to my Reiki Tummo book). The Open Heart path does not discuss energy channeling even though at the fourth level, you will learn to let True Source Love help in healing yourself. Regardless of which path you choose, you will learn how to become True Source instrument to share True Source Love with others and to activate the inner heart.

When you reach the spiritual retreat level, the two paths unite and we will begin to discuss the journey that the various human consciousnesses have gone through and the true purpose of life. You will not simply listen to stories about this, but you will be invited to feel for yourself with your inner heart, not only to simply feel but so everyone can start to "remember" their own journey again. As the topic of our discussion is our journey as humans, it is to help us understand what we have been through before we were born in this life.

Even though we will discuss the journeys of our higher consciousness and demonstrations will be given, you will not be told about your own journey. After you start to realize and remember the journey that your various consciousness have been through, you will have the opportunity to shift consciousness to the soul consciousness, to gain firsthand experience, and to share about your own experience and journey. This form of spirituality is not just a story but, rather, a journey that we have to go through. Even though I use the terminology "journey" here, we do not actually do anything other than accept everything as a Gift of Love from True Source. This is because True Source Love is helping with all of the instructions that cause the shift to happen, as well as in experiencing your higher consciousness.

All of the workshops are just to continuously improve the heart attitude to True Source and to surrender more and more to True Source. Hence, after sufficient preparation, having properly experienced shifting to soul consciousness several times, attending Surrendering to True Source and Deeper Surrendering to True Source workshops, as well as completing preparation to Masteryoga, you can attend the True Self Consciousness program. At this level, you will be conscious as your true self, to remember again your true self, and the journey that you have gone through, to be more in line with the true purpose of life.

The next program after True Self Consciousness is Master yoga, which has only one purpose; that is to trust and surrender to True Source to offer our whole heart and self to True Source, including the original causes of why our true self separated from True Source. And in surrendering, to accept all of True Source Love, so that True Source Love can bring us to return completely to True Source eternally.

1. Diagram of Workshop Flow

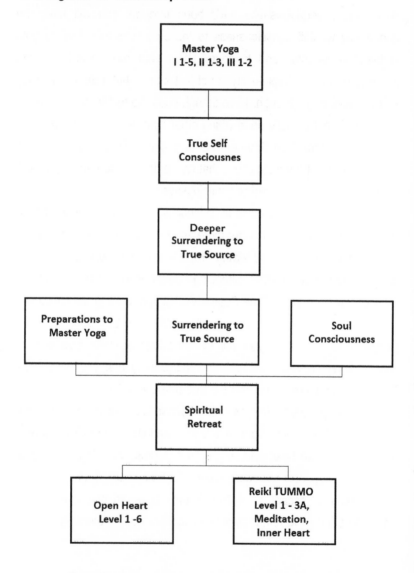

Illustration 34: Natural Way of Living Spiritual Study Flow Chart

2. Brief Description of Workshops

A. Reiki Tummo level 1-3a

1. Strengthening and Opening the Heart
2. Energy Channeling
3. Realizing that True Source is the true healer to learn to surrender to True Source in energy channeling is also beneficial in surrendering to True Source in daily life.
4. Cleansing and Opening of the Crown Chakra, the whole Sushumna and the base chakra starting from level 1.
5. At Level 3A, all main chakras are opened and the whole Sushumna is cleansed and opened more completely.

B. Meditation (Prerequisite: Reiki Tummo level 2)

1. Cleansing of the non-physical body layers
2. Sharing True Source Love to all beings

C. Kundalini (Prerequisite: Reiki Tummo level 2)

Techniques for further cleansing and purification.

D. Inner Heart (Prerequisite: Reiki Tummo level 2)

1. Letting True Source Love bring our whole heart and self within True Source Love.
2. Inner Heart as director to realize truths from our own inner Heart

E. Open Heart levels 1-6

1. Strengthening, opening and using the heart

2. Letting True Source Love bring you into True Source Love in your daily life.

3. Feeling the feeling of your heart and how to let your heart surrender more to True Source.

4. Level 4 includes how to let True Source Love help with our own health.

5. Levels 5-6 are to share True Source Love with all beings and Kundalini Awakening.

6. Level 6 includes inner heart as director to realize truths from our own inner Heart.

F. Spiritual Retreat

1. All the discussions are done interactively with participants feeling with their own inner heart.

2. Discussions about the various human consciousnesses: brain, soul, spirit, and their journeys.

3. Recognizing the true purpose of life from different perspectives. The real meaning from the perspective of the inner heart and the true purpose of life and the real meaning and true purpose of life.

4. Realizing the way to start using our lives as a facility to start directing ourselves to the true purpose of life.

G. Soul Consciousness

Letting True Source Love help us shift to our soul consciousness and personally experience what our soul has experienced. This is completely different from hypnosis. Higher consciousness means that the daily consciousness is still conscious, but at the same time there is a higher consciousness that would normally be blocked, but that can now be accessed. It is very important to recognize our soul, the weaknesses and the habits that still remain. By relying on True Source Love, our problems and weaknesses can be helped by True Source Love immediately.

H. Preparation to Master Yoga

Cleansing of the chakras and other parts of our being for further preparation, just by praying to rely on True Source Love.

I. Mastering Reiki Tummo

Even though the title is "Mastering Reiki Tummo", actually it is for all participants who began with either the Reiki Tummo path or the Open Heart path. This is to recognize the habits that make us limit True Source Love. By improving those weaknesses and habits, our heart attitude, that is our surrendering to True Source, will **improve significantly.**

J. Mastering Reiki Tummo ++

1. Digging deeper into the attitudes and habits that hold True Source Love.
2. Improving heart attitude and surrendering to True Source.

K. True Self Consciousness

1. Reaching the True Self consciousness is to realize again times when we were only the true self and the journey that we have been through so far.
2. To improve the attitude and relationship between our true self and True Source, the Source and Destiny of all humans' true self.

L. Master Yoga I 1-5, II 1-3, III 1-2

To trust and surrender to True Source completely.

Further Information

From Concept to Experiencing Love and Connection

Many people who read **Smile to Your Heart Meditation: Simple Practices for Peace, Health, and Spiritual Growth** were pleasantly surprised to see how deep their experience was in their first two-day Open Heart workshop. They said that the book was only a fraction of the real thing and did not prepare them for the real experience with their own heart. If you like the information I have shared with you in this book, I invite you to take one weekend off to experience opening your heart and to feel the real, beautiful connection that you have with the Source of whom you really are. You have heard over and over again about our heart being the key to our connection to True Source. It is now time to actually experience your heart yourself. You will be guided by the instructor in relaxing, touching your heart, smiling sweetly and freely, making it easy for you to enjoy the experience as you no longer need to

216

read, record, and listen to your own recording, and guide yourself. Some participants from these workshops have been kind enough to share their experiences some of which I shared with you at the end of the previous chapter.

The Real Path of the real purpose of life is only True Source Love, and our only True Teacher is True Source. The workshops and retreats I offer are simply facilities to help us to strengthen and use our heart - the only part of us that can accept True Source Love. Because our worldly education system (schools) focuses on brain power and not on strengthening the beautiful feelings from our heart, we need to remember how to allow our heart to be open and free. So that we can go beyond beautiful words, ideas and concepts about the Creator/God/True Source and True Source Love and start experiencing the reality of being loved and taken care of by True Source.

Because attaining the real purpose of life is infinitely deep and we want to go beyond mere theory, the workshops and retreats are designed to start with strengthening and using of our heart. Then we go deeper into spirituality at the level of the spiritual retreat, followed by reaching our soul consciousness, and then reaching our true self consciousness at the True Self retreat. Guidance, explanation, and demonstrations are given in the workshops and the retreats, but each individual will not be told their own journey. It is about realizing for oneself through Inner Heart as director what one needs to realize.

The workshops start out with a set of Reiki TUMMO® workshops and/ or a set of Open Heart workshops. In the Reiki TUMMO® workshops, participants strengthen and use their hearts through energy channeling and start to share True Source Love as instruments. In Open Heart workshops, participants strengthen and use their hearts directly without energy channeling and also start sharing the Love as instruments. These two workshop sets complement each other: Open Heart (OH) participants who later on took Reiki TUMMO® (RT) said that the energy channeling helps them feel fresher and rejuvenated when meditating, and they can feel their hearts open even more through energy channeling. RT participants, who later on took OH, said that they are able to feel the nice, beautiful feelings from their hearts more and find themselves prioritizing the Love over physical sensations from energy channeling effortlessly and yet simultaneously find better results in their energy channeling.

Once participants have experienced the beauty of opening their hearts to True Source, they often want more. Through their own experience, they appreciate that there is so much more to realize. They realize that they can still trust True Source more, surrender to True Source more, be grateful to True Source more, etc. but that only their heart with Inner Heart as director can do all these properly. Then, in the next level–Spiritual Retreat–participants are invited to use the core of their heart, their Inner Heart, the spark of True Source, to feel the journey that human consciousnesses have gone through so that they remember for themselves the real purpose of their lives.

At Spiritual Retreat, more demonstrations are given and participants are invited to watch and follow using their heart with Inner Heart as director. After using Inner Heart as director, realizations become very different from just reading about the real purpose of life: a realization from the heart/Inner Heart makes this important matter very clear, very real, very meaningful, and very beautiful.

After Spiritual Retreat (SR), to realize the real purpose of this temporary life better, SR participants can become more trusting and surrender better to True Source by letting the Love help them shift to a higher consciousness (soul consciousness) to experience it for themselves and to be the one describing their own experience. This is a big shift because, after all, spirituality is not a story that we need to know but a journey we need to take. With True Source Love as the Path and with True Source as the True Guide, we are actually not the one doing any of this; we are simply accepting Gifts of Love from True Source. Even in shifting to our soul consciousness, it is all True Source Love that is helping us.

After properly experiencing being a soul several times to realize the journey we have gone through in a much deeper way and after taking the Mastering Reiki TUMMO® (MRT) workshop, MRT++, and preparation to Masteryoga where our heart attitude is helped by the Love to improve, participants can reach their true self consciousness. Here they experience themselves as spirits/their true selves, including what they have gone through in this journey and realizing even more completely the real purpose of our life.

In addition to the straightforward purpose of the curriculum to attain the real purpose of life, because we still have to take care of our worldly responsibilities, we can start using these duties as beautiful facilities to choose and prioritize True Source after the foundation has been laid properly. This can happen once we are able to feel the beautiful feelings from the heart, having experienced being loved and taken care of by True Source, and are willing to start living our life for the real purpose of life. It is much easier to hear "Worrying about your financial situation doesn't help" or "relax and smile to accept True Source Love to let the Love work" once you have felt what we experience in Spiritual Retreat, Open Heart level 4 or level 6. This is why SR and OH4 are the minimum requirements to attend Secrets of Abundant Wealth and Happiness workshop where we move away from fretting, worrying, and working hard based on our limitations to trusting and surrendering to True Source with the Unlimited Love removing the karma that all this time has been blocking the wealth, prosperity and joy that we are supposed to receive from our beloved True Source.

There is no denying that physical discomfort can distract us from going deep into the experience of being loved and taken care of by True Source. In addition to Reiki TUMMO® where there is energy channeling, there is also the Secrets of Natural Walking® Workshop (SONW) where we remember how to use our step properly in the way we were created, so that whenever we walk our physical health can improve. After SONW and Spiritual Retreat, we will be able to surrender to True Source further in the Heart and Health Retreat. All physical improvements not only help us in our daily life but also help to open our heart further to True Source for the real purpose of life.

Being grateful to True Source is a very important key in the spiritual journey. The Grateful Retreat is where we let the Love help improve our heart attitude towards True Source so that we can be grateful to True Source in every moment of our life, giving us a beautiful and meaningful life while getting closer and closer to True Source.

Please do not be overwhelmed by the workshop and retreat information. I repeat, to attain the real purpose of life in this lifetime after our spirit left True Source and continued to reject True Source Love over many lifetimes is a process. If you are interested in any of the workshops, just allocate one weekend at a time and live your daily life more joyfully and gratefully. This way, as you experience your heart accepting the Love and your spirit really getting closer to True Source with every workshop set that you take, you will be where you need to be before you know it.

For More Information
www.naturalwayofliving.com

Note of Appreciation

In addition to my deepest gratitude to True Source for all the Gifts of Love I have received in completing this book that it may reach all of you, I also wish to take this opportunity to express my appreciation to the following individuals for their contributions:

- Damar Permono in helping to create the majority of the illustrations
- Kim Iskandar in translating the book
- Lucy Surya in formatting the book
- Krissan Iskandar in formatting the book and designing the cover
- Yalda Cassidy, Tim Johnson, Enrico Iskandar, Melky Herlina and Sandra Zein in proofreading the book

Other Books by the Author

1. Smile to your heart: Simple Meditations for Peace, health and Spiritual Growth, 2010
2. Real You: Beyond Forms and Lives, 2012
3. Kundalini: Teknik Efektif untuk Membangkitkan, Membersihkan dan Memurnikan Kekuatan Luar Biasa dalam Diri Anda, 1998. (In Indonesian) *Kundalini: An Effective Technique to Awaken, Cleanse and Purify the Extraordinary Power within, 1998*
4. Reiki: Teknik Efektif untuk Membangkitkan Kemampuan Penyembuhan Luar Biasa Secara Seketika, 1999. (In Indonesian)*Reiki: An Effective Technique to Instantaneously Awaken a Powerful Healing Ability, 1999*
5. Reiki 2: Pemantapan dan Pemanfaatan dalam Hidup sehari-hari, 1999. (In Indonesian) *Reiki 2: Mastering and Practicing in Daily Life, 1999*
6. Lima Gerakan Awet Muda Tibet (Edisi Revisi): Teknik Efektif untuk Meraih Kebugaran, Mempertahankan Keremajaan, dan Menghambat Proses Penuaan, 2012. (In Indonesian) *Five Rejuvenating Tibetan Movements (Revised Edition): An Effective Technique to Reach Fitness, Maintaining Youth and Stopping the Ageing Process, 2012*
7. Kundalini 2: Pendalaman dan Teknik Lanjutan, 2000. (In Indonesian) *Kundalini 2: A Deeper Discussion and More Advanced Techniques, 2000*

8. Reiki Tummo: Teknik Efektif untuk Meningkatkan Kesadaran dan Energi Spiritual, 2001. (In Indonesian) *Reiki Tummo: An Effective Technique to Increase Awareness and Spiritual Energy, 2001*

9. Hati Nurani, 2002. (In Indonesian) *Inner Heart, 2002*

10. Mencapai Tujuan Hidup yang Sebernarnya, 2003. (In Indonesian) *Attaining the True Purpose of Life, 2003*

11. Reiki Tummo: An Effective Technique for Health and Happiness, 2004

12. Seri Hati Dan Kasih: Akal Budi, 2007 (In Indonesian) *Heart and Love Series: Mind and Conscience, 2007*

13. Heart and Love Series: Sweetheart, 2007 (Translation in English from Indonesian)

14. Serie Herz und Liebe: Süsse Herz, 2007 (Translation in German from Indonesian)

15. Serie Corazon y Amor: Dulce Corazon, 2008 (Translation in Spanish from Indonesian)

16. Hati: Mengenal, membuka dan memanfaatnya, 2013 (Revised Edition) (In Indonesian) Heart: Getting acquainted, Opening and Benefiting from and Open Heart

17. Menuai Hasil dalam Reiki: Teknik Mengoptimalkan Energi Reiki Secara Luar Biasa, 2009 (In Indonesian) Reaping Results in Reiki: A Technique to Optimize Reiki Energy Extraordinarily, 2009

18. Kesadaran Jiwa: Teknik Efektif untuk Mencapai Kesadaran yang Lebih Tinggi (Revisi Tambahan: Metode Perpindahan Kesadaran), 1999, 2009. (In Indonesian) Soul Consciousness: An Effective Technique to Reach your Higher Consciousness (Additional Revision: Consciousness Shifting Method), 1999, 2009

19. Shing Chi: Teknik Efektif untuk Mengakses Energi Ilahi (Edisi Revisi),

2009 (In Indonesian) Shing Chi: An Effective Technique to Access Divine Energy (Revised Edition), 2009

20. Rahasia Berjalan Alami: Aktifkan Kemampuan Penyembuhan Luar Biasa Tubuh Anda, 2016 (In Indonesian) Secrets of Natural Walking® (SONW): Activate the Extraordinary Healing Capabilities of Your Body, 2016

About the Author

Irmansyah Effendi graduated with a Bachelor of Science in Computer Science and Mathematics at the age of 20 with magna cum laude and honor from California State University, United States. He graduated with a Master of Science, majoring in Computer Science and specializing in Artificial Intelligence at the age of 21 from the same university.

After reaching his true self consciousness, he realized how True Source loves and takes care of all beings completely, always wants to help, guide, and give the best. That are the ones who are still too busy with our own wants and personal needs. He realised that in praying to True Source, we are usually busy with our wants and needs and not using our heart or inner heart. He also understood that we usually remember and pray to True Source, not for True Source, but for ourselves, for instance to go to heaven, for our earthly needs, etc.

After this, Irmansyah introduced Open Heart prayer, which is nondenominational. Open Heart prayer invites everyone to strengthen and open their hearts to True Source so that they can realize more clearly how True Source really loves and takes care of us all and so that they can trust and surrender more to True Source allowing True Source Love to give us the most beautiful and wonderful things on earth and the afterlife. Irmansyah Effendi has shared with thousands worldwide that prosperity, health and joy are all part of True Source unlimited gifts of love for you, and we need to remember that our lives are just facilities to be closer to True Source.

Lightning Source UK Ltd.
Milton Keynes UK
UKHW041820261018
331273UK00001B/54/P